WOLF

A STORY OF HATE

ZEEV SCHEINWALD
ELLA SCHEINWALD

Wolf. A Story of Hate by Zeev Scheinwald

Transcribed and translated by Ella Scheinwald

Preface by Ella Scheinwald

ISBN: 9789493056442 (ebook)

ISBN: 9789493056435 (paperback)

Copyright © Ella Scheinwald, 2020

Publisher: Amsterdam Publishers

All Rights Reserved. No part of this publication may be reproduced or transmitted in any form or by any means, electronic or mechanical, including photocopy, recording or any other information storage and retrieval system, without prior permission in writing from the publisher.

CONTENTS

Preface	v
Introduction	xi
Wolf	1
Epilogue	223
Afterword	227
Bibliography	229
Photos	231
About the Authors	243

PREFACE

This is the biography of a murdered person.

He was murdered by normal people. By people who had wives, husbands, children, parents. People who were often nice and had the capacity to love.

But this is not just a story about the Holocaust, or one person's experience of it. This is a much bigger story, one that resonates with our times, that is relevant to all of us, today. It reverberates in how some countries are being led today, including modern cultures, democracies, as well as developed and underdeveloped countries. Among others, it is the story of how political and industrial leadership fails their own purposefully, by creating profound divisions filling people's hearts and minds with hate beyond comprehension, with not an eye blinked by entire populations who have lost their moral compass, or are blindsided and ignorant to the point of indifference. When some blame Jews for going to the gas chambers like cattle, it is merely a projection of the behavior of most of the local non-Jewish population in Germany and its allies who ignored the plight and suffering of their countrymen and followed their own regimes like ignorant cattle. Even today, people often misconstrue their government as a body which defends the country's own interests, when in fact, leadership itself reaps all the financial and political benefits.

This is the story of the relationship between government and corporations, alliances between regimes and businesses, marriages between politics and industries, and how innocent human beings get trapped in an evil circle of fanaticism, political polarization, manipulation of admiring masses, exploitation and divisiveness. Exploiting innocent people can quickly plunge into an abyss of hate and genocide.

These relationships do not only exist "elsewhere". Germans were considered a highly cultured people before Hitler came to power. It did not take much to turn Germany, the Germans and their allies into a death enterprise. Hate was it.

In an article from the New York Magazine (January 6-19, 2020) entitled "What will happen to the Trump Toadies? Look to Nixon's defenders, and the Vichy collaborators, for clues", the writer Frank Rich says: "More than half-century after V-E Day, researchers confirmed that Ford and GM's German operations had manufactured armaments for the Nazi war machine, sometimes with slave labor. Alfred P. Sloan, the longtime GM chairman, explained his philosophy: 'An international business operating throughout the world should conduct its operations in strictly business terms, without regard to the political beliefs of its management, or the political beliefs of the countries in which it is operating.'" He adds: "Newly discovered documents, triggered in part by litigation on behalf of Holocaust survivors, would show, as the Washington Post put it, that in consultation with Göring, "he was involved in the partial conversion of the principal GM automobile plant at Russelsheim to production of engines and other parts for the Junker 'Wunderbomber', a key weapon in the German air force."

While my father was not in a GM or Ford connected camp, he was used as slave in HASAG-owned camps, a company that had alliances with the murderous Nazi regime, turning it to a de facto death corporation. Hate became the medium through which everything was justified. Politics of hate, business of hate, genocide of hate – they all spiraled down and snowballed to a state of collective hate trance.

My father Wolf, like millions of others, fell victim to this trance under the watchful eye of entire populations, businesses and politicians, all morally bankrupt and self-serving.

Imagine how much better the world would be if all these beautiful human beings were not victims of this mass murder.

I had to detach myself from the narrative when I co-wrote and translated this biography. Yet, how could I deal with this kind of material knowing that every line has shaped my own life? Through the words, I got to meet part of the family I never had. I encountered little Bela, whose big, dark eyes often look at me at night. For a fleeting moment, I got to meet the grandparents, uncles and aunts I never had in life.

When I agreed to visit Poland for the first time in the early 1990s, I could only see a land where countless Jews are buried. Not because they died of natural causes, but because they were murdered. Poland is a big cemetery. Its soil is soaked with the blood of its Jewish citizens – men, women, children – and the blood has not yet dried on the hands of the perpetrators.

If my father had not accompanied me on this visit, I would have never found any memorial or sign of what had happened there.

The Poles achieved their dream: the land is Judenrein – free of Jews – but not free of antisemitism. It is still burning in their hearts and flows in many mothers' milk.

I saw a land wooed by the world's politicians and businesspeople, some even Jewish, hungry for money, ignoring an uneasy past for the sake of profit. I also saw a people capitalizing on their own collaboration by making those who experienced the camps pay to see them once more. Many asked me: why do you need to write all of this? Why are you still angry? Forget it, go on with your life.

Well, this is my life. I live with the Holocaust because I am a product of it. I agreed to do this work because my father asked me to. We wanted to listen to him, to understand and help him, but we could not make him happy. Even the presence of grandchildren has not made up for his losses and loneliness. He remained a shell of a person, a body emptied of joy and freedom through torture and death.

A murdered person.

Finally, while I may disagree with my father regarding certain opinions and conclusions relating to his writings, it does not come from a place of judgement or criticism, but rather it is based on the fantasy of a better and more caring world. It is crucial to remember that he was persecuted by the Nazis and their co-conspirators, and that his entire family and community were destroyed. Regardless, I remained completely loyal to what he asked me to write and to the translation of his manuscript.

I dedicate this book to my children, Ronen and Dana, with my deepest love and respect.

Ella Scheinwald

INTRODUCTION

On May 4, 1945, as I was lying on a wooden board in one of Mauthausen's barracks, on the verge of death, only hours before I was freed by American forces, I started thinking about how to describe what had happened to us here. I soon realized that it was an obligation to write it all down. As you can see, it took me many years before I was able to do so, and even now it is not easy. I have decided to tell most of my story, and only things I witnessed myself. It is all authentic and first-hand. There are no other witnesses and no official archives recording what happened. Most of the would-be witnesses are no longer among the living.

This is an account of the small, corporate-owned labor death camps. I want to tell what has not been sufficiently told before and what might never have been truthfully told in the future.

It is also a tale of abandonment and treason.

The real nature of the small camps is often ignored. These camps were forced labor camps, were very small, and contained relatively few people. There were no gas chambers or crematoria to burn women, children and old people. But the suffering we endured was agonizing and traumatic, and as painfully difficult as in the large camps. Often it was even more unbearable.

It is my duty to write what I know.

Future generations must know what the murderous German people and their co-conspirators did to us. The world must beware of such evil in the future. Each person must see it as a sacred obligation to always remember what they did to us, and not allow them to resort to excuses such as that it happened in darker times, and that they therefore cannot be held responsible for these actions. If people accept this argument, they will do the same again. When a new dictator rises, they will do worse things too, if possible.

Germans were militaristic by nature and character and tended to embrace dictatorships; this was quite obvious preceding and during World War Two. The great majority of Austrians also fulfilled their duty in this cruel war and took part in the murders, just as their countryman Hitler was expecting them to do. Their guilt is no lesser than that of the Germans.

After the war, the world rewarded them, gave them independence, and decreed they had been a country under occupation. What a lie and what a disgrace.

As we were rotting away, abandoned by the world and our own leadership, we had no clue we were unimportant. We thought someone was desperately trying to save us.

Some Jewish leaders could have helped but chose instead to flee or commit suicide. Other world leaders simply ignored our plight because of antisemitism, including the American administration.

I feel shame to have had such "leaders" in Palestine and throughout the world. I feel sad to know that the Americans, through their silence and inaction, agreed to watch the massacre of innocent people. And so did the Catholic church, which for generations groomed its followers to hate.

I hope you will read this book and that you will learn from it. Maybe it will help raise awareness so that you will do your best to make sure no such atrocities ever happen again.

I wish you success.

WOLF

A STORY OF HATE

As I see it today, Sochaczew is a large village, or a little town, and it is dirty and neglected. But this is not how I perceived it as a child.

Sochaczew was my birthplace, and the birthplace of my parents and their parents. My great-grandparents were the first generation in my family to move to "the city". I am not quite sure where they moved from. I believe that my father's side originated in Germany, my last name being German, and my mother's side was Polish. Today, I am not proud of either origin. But as a child growing up in that small town, I was very proud of both my parents, and I was convinced that I was living in the happiest household of all time, in a city close to Warsaw, the capital, and that the earth was revolving around Sochaczew.

I thought that at the smallest tremor in Sochaczew, the whole world would collapse and that everyone, across the universe, knew of every detail and was concerned about everything that went on in Poland, especially in my hometown, and its close neighbor to the East, the capital. After all, it was only a 50-kilometer (31-mile) trip by horse-drawn carriage that took a whole night to cover the distance away. Even winter temperatures that reached 20 to 30 degrees below zero were nothing compared to the greatness of being so closely connected with Poland's capital. Jews had been living there for over 600 years and were an inherent part of life in this center of the universe. Or so I thought.

Sochaczew is one of the oldest cities in Mazowsze or Congressional Poland (all of Warsaw and its surroundings are called Mazowsze, meaning congressional). During 1,000 years of Poland's history and all its repartitions following wars between Russia, Germany, Austria, Lithuania, Sweden and Prussia, the town Sochaczew and Mazowsze always remained in their entirety as a central part of Poland.

There are no details as to when Jews began settling in Sochaczew, but it is clear beyond any doubt that in the period 1426-1455 Jews became landowners, and it is highly likely they had arrived in Sochaczew many years earlier (see Gabriel Weissman in *Sochaczew Journal*, 1962, in Yiddish). The first Jews who moved from Warsaw to Sochaczew came after a Jewish cemetery had been delineated. They would bring the dead to bury. When in 1887 the local church was being refurbished, early documents were found, including one reading "here lies the bones of a little girl who was murdered by the Jews on July 12, 1617". This was a very difficult time for Jews, but they still did not leave, nor did they abandon the town during other harsh periods; there were occasional wars above the river Bzura, usually ending up destroying the town. The history of Sochaczew Jews therefore covers 600 years, and in 1941, they accounted for 85% of the population in the town.

During my last few visits to Sochaczew, the Bzura looked more like a stinking sewer than a river due to the nearby industrial manufacturing plants. When I was a child, the river seemed clean, and we would swim in it in the summer, and play, and have fun. Until the late 1920s, we would also drink the river's water, and use it for all household purposes. Some people supported their families by bringing water in pails from the river to people's houses. Of course, without water, there were no modern toilets, but there was an outhouse that all the neighbors used. It was no fun waiting to use it, and it was a hardship to get up at night, especially in the winter. So in those days, we used bed pans. Sometimes there was so much snow that we could not get out of the house at all. The caretaker (known in Polish as Dozorca) had to shovel meters and meters of snow in order to get the doors to open. During these cold days, we had much fun inside the house.

I lived with my parents, siblings, and my grandfather. All in all, there would be ten people stuck in the apartment and for us children, it was heaven. I can now imagine the level of "fun" my parents experienced, having all the children stuck at home... the minute the doors opened, someone would rush out for bread, especially freshly baked rolls which we would purchase from the bakery across the unpaved road, and the milkman would deliver fresh milk, and for us, it was all a big party.

During the rainy months, following winter, we would get soaked and water would filter in through our shoes when we played outside in the rain and the mud. We would make mud cakes, get our clothes dirty, and tease people who used the toilets.

There was a neighbor who suffered from a hernia. Sometimes, when we knew he was using the outhouse, we would take a stick, at the end of which we would hammer in a nail, and we would push the stick under the toilet door and try to tickle him with the nail. We were young kids, and we wanted to play and laugh. There was not even a park in town, so we had to be creative.

During the summer, we played outside all the time, inventing games and arguing with one another. For example, we would try to catch bugs and worms. I remember particularly a game that we invented, and which we often played by the outhouse. We would catch the biggest flies we could find, the bigger and more colorful the better, and we would stick them in a matchbox or a jar (in our eyes, a child with a jar was a wealthy kid). We would tear their wings off, push a short straw into their bodies, and after we had placed them on a starting line, the flies would compete in a long-distance run. The kid with the fastest fly would win whatever it was we had agreed upon, maybe another fly or a button, sometimes a coin. Of course, we children did not realize how unhygienic and cruel that game was; everyone around us was inventing similar games. When we came home, my mother would get angry at us for being filthy, but we were kids, we had little else to do, and we were happy with our games and fun.

When I was a little older, we started playing soccer. We would place two stones to delineate the gate, but we had no ball. Instead we would gather rags and pieces of rope and wire, forming a sphere out of these components. It hardly looked like a ball, but we felt like world champions in our home field, and it was great.

Games and fun were for after school and Sundays, except that the Poles were at church that day. There was no playing between Friday evening and Sunday morning, of course.

Since I was a little Jewish boy, I had to go to the Cheder to learn the Torah. At the Cheder, which was close to my house – what wasn't – there was a teacher Rabbi, the Melamed Gedalihu. We called him Gedalkele Fortz, meaning fart. He was a short man, maybe five feet; tall as a fart, we thought. People were often called by their nicknames, which were given to them based on their attributes. My paternal grandfather's name was Yossel the Blind. He was not blind at all, he had excellent vision, except for a slight defect in one of his eyes.

I started learning the Alef-Beit with Gedalkele Fortz when I was four. We were seated in a small room of about twenty square meters that served as kitchen, living room and bedroom. It was also where one of his sons manufactured paper bags for grocery stores. Fifteen to twenty kids would be seated around a table studying the Torah. When I turned six, my teacher was Jacob, nicknamed Yankele, and he was somehow related to me. He taught in a room separated from the main living quarters, and our learning experience there was more serious and more difficult. He taught Humash, Rashi and Gemara, and he would walk around the room wielding a whip. He would use it on students who did not know the right answers, or who did not understand the lesson. He would test us at the end of every week, and if we did not know our lesson, we would have to study all of Sunday. On Saturdays, my father would test me, and grandfather would also ask me questions to see what I had retained from the lesson. At seven, I was sent to the regular public elementary school, and every afternoon, after school, I would return to the Cheder for Judaic studies.

One day, I found a tomato. I did not know what it was, so I asked my father. He said I had to check with the Rabbi who in turn proclaimed the tomato was treif, meaning not Kosher. That made it too much of a temptation for me. I sank my teeth in the tomato, its juice running down my lips and chin, and to this day I remember the sweetness of it. My father, who agreed with the Rabbi about the tomato's status as a non-Kosher food, was very unhappy about my behavior.

Elementary school was hard. Not because of the content of the lessons, but because the Jewish children had not attended pre-school or kindergarten and were not ready for secular studies in the Polish public schools. We had spent our days at the Cheder from the age of four. I remember being jealous of children who went to the only nursery school in town.

Even in first grade, Polish children would tease Jewish kids in school. Their meanness increased as the years went by. They had a problem with us not eating pork. Once a bunch of Polish boys caught a Jewish kid, a blond, blue-eyed boy who was perhaps six or seven years old, cut off one of his peyes sidelocks and forced pork into his mouth. For his family, this was an act of incomparable cruelty. The Polish boys only laughed, cheered on by their parents and their priest.

Later the Polish children would remark that we had "killed" Jesus and express their desire that we leave and go away to Palestine, not understanding even themselves what they were talking about, just repeating what they kept hearing at home. Then they started beating us up. The school administration always took their side. Sometimes the beatings were so bad that the police had to be called in. They would side with the abusers. We, Jews, had no rights, and were made to feel like unwanted foreigners, and none of the Poles minced words about it. On Sundays, we would sometimes go to soccer games held by the Jewish organization Zydowski Towazytwo Gimnastyczno Sportwe – ZTGS – who played against a socialist Polish team. Whether we won or lost, we would get beaten up at the end of the game. They would throw stones at the players, and at us, the audience, and the police would join them in their abusive fun. Antisemitism in Poland before the war needed no explanation. They were born with it, they hated us, and they implemented their hate to the maximum. This hatred is prevalent even today in Poland, although there are no Jews there to speak of. It is inexplicable, but antisemitism is simply part of their worldview.

When I grew up, my parents moved me to a Jewish school where I started learning Hebrew. Life at home was not easy, although we were all close to one another and had good relationships with each other. When my maternal grandparents, Avraham and Bela, were alive, they lived close by and served as a magnet for the whole family. We would meet there on Saturdays after synagogue where we all prayed with Saba, grandpa. After a festive lunch, we would rest and gather again at their house with my uncles Israel, Shlomo and Hersh and my aunt Haya. I do not remember anyone ever being absent from these family gatherings except for one uncle, Louis, who had moved to the United States. We would walk over to my grandparents' house where plenty of food and drink awaited us. There were always many children of all ages – the grandchildren – running around happily, making noise and creating chaos.

The adults would talk about the Torah, and would discuss politics, recent events and local gossip. My grandparents' house was later burned down by the Germans, and they were buried in a Jewish cemetery the Germans and Poles destroyed, which I tried to restore and give some dignity to with a memorial many years later.

Despite the difficult living conditions many Sochaczew Jews endured, and there was a vibrant cultural life. There was a theater, there were many synagogues, social and cultural centers, and intellectuals who would organize lectures and discussions for all to attend.

At my parents' house there was always food. Clothing was passed down from one child to the next and we did not want for anything. We were not wealthy, but we managed. Father worked hard to support us. At some point in the 1920s, he was recruited by the military. I remember Mother crying and wondering what to do. When he returned, he was ill and had to be hospitalized in Warsaw for two weeks. He then suffered a hemorrhage and never fully recovered.

Later, Mother got sick with arthritis, and at a relatively young age, she could no longer walk around freely and became chairbound. Around that time, my brother Hersh was drafted into the Polish cavalry but returned after fleeing from a German POW camp.

In the meantime, we were reasonably happy. We thought we had it all, not realizing we had very little.

Electricity was connected to the house at end of the 1920s or early in the 1930s, but we did not have running water. At some point, water pipes were installed, and pumps were placed in the town's three squares. We were informed not to drink the river water, but many people complained that the new machinery was making the water taste like asphalt, but we all got used to that too. Many people lived in utter poverty, and in unbearable conditions; many could not afford to buy coal for heating and some did not have enough food to feed their children. Given this context, we lived relatively well. We would get new clothing for the holidays, and close to the outbreak of the war, Father considered buying a house, or at least changing apartments. But the war preceded him.

The period between November 11, 1918 and September 27, 1939 was an uneasy time for Polish Jews because at the beginning of 1918 the pogroms started. General Józef Haller was famous for it. He had a military division that he used to attack and kill Jews. Jews were afraid of Hallerschiks, as they were called, and when I was a child, I knew I had to avoid them. Later on, Polish Jews were victims of antisemitism during the 1920s when the economist Władysław Dominik Grabski, who destroyed the economy after the Polish independence, was "accused" of being a Jew. Although that was untrue, the Jews paid a high price.

Then, an anti-Semitic bill advocating the forbidding of Kosher animal slaughter was presented to the Polish House of Parliament, describing the practice as immoral. When the head of state Slawoj Skladkowski was scolded for not physically attacking Jews, he responded by saying that if people wanted to boycott against Jews, they should do it: "Bojkot? Owszem" (Boycott? Fine). He did not suggest that people kill Jews, so therefore Jewish businesses were boycotted. His words led to physical attacks against Jews anyway.

Jews had to guard their stores, and any Pole who dared to shop in Jewish stores would have a badge posted on their coat, like a sticker, that read: this pig buys in Jewish shops. That hurt some Polish peasants, who did not understand why they had to walk with stickers on their backs. They were initially puzzled as to why they should not shop at Jewish stores, when their parents and grandparents did business with Jews. Where else should they buy? There was no Polish trade. The few stores owned by Poles were more expensive. People were expected to pay more, to support Polish trade and destroy Jewish businesses.

They stuck billboards everywhere. The people leading the

charge received police protection and support from the justice system. There was no one to protect us. Even our closest "friends" were openly anti-Semitic and against us. They simply hated Jews. Not all Poles felt that way, however, no one stood up on our behalf or was sorry for our fate. The good souls remained passive and silent. Very few were prepared to help us, and those who were had no power anyway and protected themselves first. What can you expect from a people hearing anti-Semitic messages from their leaders and who have a natural propensity for hate to begin with? This situation came to be despite the fact that Jews served in the military and in every war had sacrificed themselves for Poland. When this war erupted, and they started calling the reserves, billboards were stuck on walls calling on Poles to protect their homeland. Jews were imprisoned and were sent to jail until they were forced to "contribute" money which they lacked in the form of bribes. Even if they paid, many Jews still died in prison.

The Polish masses were highly influenced by young anti-Semites. As people worked together digging shelters against air raids, they would say things like "just wait, Hitler will come and teach you it is not worth being a Jew; he will kill you, he will teach you a lesson". In their eyes it was not significant that Hitler would also conquer them and kill millions of Poles, as long as he killed us Jews.

Indeed, when Poland was conquered more Poles could have helped but they did not. Those who were willing were afraid because of informers. With thirty million people in Poland, if only 1% had saved Jews, can one imagine what number that would have represented? Instead, they formed partisan groups called Armja Krajowa – or AK – which were dedicated to the murder of Jews who managed to escape the ghettos during and before the killings and make it into the forests. The AK, instead of fighting with us against the Germans, killed Jews themselves, or gave them away to the Germans, and were busy sending informers to every city. Often, someone would inform for a bottle of vodka or a kilo of sugar. Our life among the Poles was cheap. Even if some Poles jeopardized their lives and hid Jews, there were too few of them and many of them did it for money or romantic love. Many paid with their lives because of the informers. Sodom and Gomorra.

On Friday September 1, 1939, we woke up to a new dawn: the dawn of war. From early morning we would hear sirens and see German fighter planes on their way to bomb Warsaw. Like many others, we were sure they would not destroy such a large and beautiful city and moved from the surrounding areas into the capital. Evidently, we were clueless as to the Germans' plans and frame of mind. Thus, those who fled towards Warsaw ran straight into bombings, heavy artillery and fires that destroyed a large part of the city before it was finally conquered.

My family found shelter at a friend's apartment on 12 Grzybowska Street. One day, the house was hit and burned down. We were cowering in the basement without food. Father suggested that we go out to look for something to eat. When, for a brief moment, the bombings stopped, we ventured out. A short distance from us, a boy of about 12 years was also looking for food in the ruins. Or maybe he wanted to play. As we slowly advanced on the pavement, I saw, in a spilt second, the boy's body cut in two. Simultaneously, I heard an explosion. I understood that a shell had hit him. It had gone through the church steeple, broken the cross on Grzybowski Place and continued straight into this kid. He was the first dead person I saw in the war.

I do not know where his parents were, or even who they were, I can only guess that they waited for their child to return. But he never returned home. What grief his parents must have felt not knowing why he never came back, and why they would never see him again. Perhaps he was their only child.

At that time, I still had a family. A mother, Lea, and a father, Moshe – both born in 1889. I had brothers and sisters. Hersh was 22 at the time, Rachel 16, Feige 14, Haim 12, Jacob 10, and Bela 7. In the summer of 1939, I had just turned 18.

Since Warsaw was under attack, we decided to return to Sochaczew, which proved to be a tragic mistake. At the time, we did not realize the seriousness of moving back. What we should have done instead of going West back to Sochaczew was to continue East toward territories conquered by Russia. That would have allowed us to penetrate deep into Russia and perhaps kept more of us alive.

Sadly, that was not our decision then.

When we arrived, the town was already partly burned and destroyed, and our house occupied by a Polish family. We had to pay them dearly to leave, even though it was our property.

Mr. Prausse's house was untouched. Two large swastika flags were hanging from the fourth floor. He had been the town secretary until the war, and the Nazis had elected him mayor because he was a German born in Poland. It turned out that he had been spying for the Germans even before the war.

Prausse's brother had a bakery in front of which there was an endless line for bread. I, too, joined the queue, which was guarded by a German soldier. When my turn came, a "friend" called the soldier, pointed to me, and said "Jude". I was immediately taken out of the line and returned to the back. On a second attempt, I managed to get two loaves of bread for my family, a great accomplishment. Even then, bread was an expensive and important food item we dreamed about. Later on, there was no bread at all for Jews.

The Germans captured the Sochaczew Rabbi and forced him to sweep the street with his beard. They then harnessed him to a carriage like a horse and forced another Jew to take the reins and whip him. While this was going on, the town Poles laughed and spat at the two poor souls as they went past.

Following Nazi orders, the Jews and Jewish culture disappeared from Sochaczew. All that eventually remained in the town was a ruined cemetery and one Jew also named Scheinwald. We were not related, and he had converted to Christianity. Occasionally he was the target of anti-Semitic comments anyway. His household and children were Christian, but still the Poles reminded him where he came from.

In this town, where Rabbi Avramale used to live, Jewish cultural life had been thriving; intellectual circles were abundant, youth organizations active, and Torah students and Jewish life vibrant.

Never was there Jewish crime. There is no documentation regarding a single Jewish thief in the town, though it had a large Jewish population. The youth was healthy and productive.

By the time the war broke out, and the Nazis started taking measures against Jews, various signs multiplied throughout Sochaczew, warning the Poles not to conduct business with Jews and advising them to distance themselves from the Jewish community. And then some signs and billboards, initialed and written by the Poles, turned up. Some read as follows:

> *Polish peasant:*
> *Remember: when you buy in Polish stores, you help increase the number of jobs for our children. Because the villages are overflowing, they will work in trade in the big town.*
> *Remember: when you buy in Polish stores and when you sell to Poles, you help develop trade and you give financial power to the Polish people.*
> *If you want the best for your children, if you want a strong and large Poland, remember the saying: buy only in Polish stores. They are from us, for us, by us.*
>
> *The Association of Polish shopkeepers of Sochaczew.*

It was clear that Jews were not seen as being part of Polish people and targeted as the enemy.

Other signs read as follows:

> *Poles!*
> *A new year is starting in the Polish village.*
> *The war will make the Jews invade us.*
> *We will get Jews out of our villages.*
> *They are the enemy*
> *that took the proceeds from our work.*
> *People: our mission is to make our villages, which are filled with Jews, filled with Polish trade.*
> *Those who are not farmers or are unemployed will take over the work of the Jew.*
> *In this economic war against the Jew, we will give work to the Poles.*

Their true feelings towards us started emerging, with the signs getting increasingly more poisonous and laced with threats:

> *Poles from Towns and Villages!*
> *Peasants, Professionals and Shopkeepers!*
> *Do not give one cent to Jews!*
> *Polish wheat for Polish flour*
> *Agricultural products for Polish store owners*
> *Products from factories for Polish stores*
> *Those who break these rules are traitors!*
> *Fight for a Poland free of Jews, Poland for the Poles, national Poland! National!*

Jews, it appeared, with all their contributions to Polish culture, were now to be avoided and discriminated against.

> *Poles!*
> *Four million partisan Jews on account of the Poles*
> *Jews control production,*
> *trade and liberal professions*
> *Four million Jews are ready to steal money from the hard-working Polish peasant and from the Polish worker*
> *When children are hungry,*
> *you let yourself be exploited by Jews*
> *This situation must stop!*
> *You are not allowed to walk into Jewish stores*
> *You cannot buy in a Jewish store for even one cent*
> *A Pole who buys in Jewish stores is a traitor to the homeland*
> *Victory under the young Polish flag!*
> *ZMP, Sochaczew Branch*

(The texts from the signs have been translated from the *Sochaczew Journal*)

We proceeded to adapt to life under occupation. We could not fathom what that meant under Nazi Germany.

Our elders still had fresh memories of the First World War when the Germans had behaved quite differently, and when the fear was from the Russians, not the Germans. They could not imagine things being different this time. We thought of the Germans as normal, civilized people. Many Jews, just like us, returned to Sochaczew, and life continued with us managing the best we could under the new circumstances. Progressively new rules were issued by the Germans with the cooperation of the Poles and Polish bureaucracy. They detested us at least as much as the Germans did. The latter could not identify us, really; as they could not tell the difference between the Poles and Jews, they needed the Poles to point us out to them. Germans imagined us having large noses, hunched backs, long locks of hair and beards. Perhaps they thought we had horns too.

Under occupation, all schools, including Polish ones, were closed. All banks, newspapers, cultural institutions and government offices also stopped functioning.

The Germans ordered the Jewish leaders to organize a Jewish community council, later called the Judenrat. In a short period of time, this Judenrat was created and the Germans began to present their demands. They needed young, strong individuals to send to work in agriculture, dig out the city from the rubble, build an airport, a new bridge and camps, fell trees and clear fields for farming.

Is it challenging to explain what military occupation is to those who have never experienced it. It is even harder to explain what occupation under a totalitarian regime is like, especially when it includes the SS, the SD and the Gestapo as well as the

Wehrmacht. One cannot refuse to do anything under this type of occupation. They would kidnap people, or arrest them, then blackmail friends and relatives for money, manpower or any other thing they had decided they wanted. Anything they wanted done had to be carried out, or people would be put to death. Often, they would murder people at random anyway. Sometimes they would round up Jews in a synagogue and burn them alive. It was a harsh authoritarian regime ruled by violent, cruel and evil human beings. And that was just the beginning. The situation worsened minute by minute, and not one day would go by without the assassinations of Jews. There was no possibility to protest against even the tiniest of actions or decisions.

When in 1939 the Germans completed their conquest, they started "taking care" of the civilian population, meaning the elimination of the intelligentsia, particularly the Polish one, and beatings and killings increased. Their plans and goals were still unknown then, at least to us. Although some Poles were being killed, the population in general still cooperated with the Germans.

Many young Jews decided to travel towards the Eastern part of Poland, which was occupied by the Russians. I, too, joined the stream, and my brother Hersh joined me later.

We were shocked when we arrived in Bialystok. It was invaded by refugees, and there was no place to stay. It was filthy and dilapidated, whole families were living without toilets and showers. No one seemed bothered by it, and the Russians could not care less. All they were interested in was whether we came from a family of traders or laborers. Maybe, if we were capitalists, that would have made them take action, and we would have been sent directly to Siberia. Those who claimed to be communists had to return to their homes on the German side, and once there, fight for the cause. The road into Russia was blocked, except for those headed to Siberia. The Russians had no right to do this, because we were Polish citizens, but if anyone had previously owned a store, had a little money, or had ideas different from what they were supposed to believe, they were sent to Siberia.

We found a miserable place to stay with a family, but under horrible conditions, and Hersh and I realized that in light of the situation, staying in Bialystok was not an option. We heard from the Finnish front that the "Great" Russian was battling it, this crumb of a country. The Russians wanted to conquer a miniscule area there, as if all they needed in addition to their then 8,600,000 square miles (three times as large as the United States) was a tiny piece of land.

There were about four million people in Finland at the time, and it covered approximately 130,000 square miles. But the Russians suffered heavy losses, and when we saw how pitiful the Russian soldiers looked, and how they moved their supplies on carts drawn by horses with simple ropes, we realized that one does not win a war with only marches, parades and songs. We started suspecting that they would be unable to confront the Germans when the day would come. Everyone understood that war would soon break out. We also missed our family, and a letter from Father arrived indicating the situation at home was improving. The letter said that Jews were still allowed to keep a horse, and even a bicycle, and that there was sufficient food, and asked us to return home to Sochazew.

After some preparation, Hersh and I began making our way back, but were caught by the Nazis while trying to cross the border and taken to a barn that functioned as a makeshift jail.

We quickly decided to escape, and found an opportunity to do so when we were ordered to chop wood for our captors. Our goal was to escape into a forest about half a kilometer away, and from there continue home.

It was winter, and the ground was covered with heavy, wet snow, making it impossible to see if there were holes or ditches, significantly slowing our movement. The escape was difficult – our shoes quickly filled with snow and I would frequently get stuck. It got to the point that I collapsed from exhaustion. Hersh tried to encourage me, but I was too faint and had no strength. Hersh then said: "If you do not get up, they will kill us both, because I will not leave you alone here." With great determination, I got up again, and with Hersh's help made it to the forest.

After winding our way through the forest, we encountered a Pole, who gave us directions to Wegrow, a town near Treblinka. From there, it took us another two days to arrive at home.

Unfortunately, when we finally arrived at home, we were met with sadness. Our father, who had convinced us to return in his letter, was in tears. Only two days after sending the letter, all property had been confiscated from Sochaczew's Jews; they had been forced into labor, and were even forbidden from walking on the sidewalk. He cried: "Your lives are on my conscience." It was the first time I saw father cry. But now, at least, we were all together.

Shortly thereafter, the situation continued to deteriorate when the Nazis forced Sochaczew's Jews to relocate to the Warsaw Ghetto.

I was first sent to work fixing a bridge that had been blown up on a river by Debsk. It was about nine kilometers from Sochaczew.

Life was still relatively easy; nothing much had changed, and we even got paid a symbolic amount, a few pennies by today's standards. This allowed us to buy food from local peasants and bring it home on the weekends. We thought that if that was the face of German conquest, then we could bear it until the end of the war. We were hoping that the end was approaching, and that it was just a matter of months before the fighting would stop. It was a "modern" war, which for sure would not last more than six months.

France and England had already proclaimed war on Germany. There was a blockade by the British navy against the Germans, who lacked gas and should be unable to keep going for long. This theory did not even take into account Russian involvement. The Red Army was ready to crush German fascism. There was no reason for concern, everything would be fine. Amen. As we know now, that is not how things unraveled.

After the project in Debsk, we were transferred to a town named Puszcza Kampinoska. There, we saw only Jews from Sochaczew, and I was the only one from my family. We were still close to my hometown, but the conditions were different. We worked in water up to our chest building channels for draining a swamp. That area bordered Frederic Chopin's town of Zelazowa Wola. We were told that we, and the general Jewish population, would be compensated for our work.

Our situation was not easy, but the family was still together at home, and was helping one another get by. Life was not unbearable yet. But the Germans' demands escalated daily, and they started forcing young people to go to work in camps very far from their homes. There were not enough youngsters as many had fled to the Russian side.

One day, my older brother Hersh was taken along with other youngsters to work in Belzec, near Lublin. We did not know where they had been sent, and the Judenrat was not sure either. After a week or two, he managed to escape and returned home with a friend. He did not look the same; we were shocked to see his sad appearance. He told us they had received no food or water for the past weeks. He witnessed one of his friends take his hat off, wring it onto his lips and drink the water it had absorbed from the falling rain. Only later did we learn what Belzec was all about, and we understood the Germans had sent my brother and his friend to build a death camp.

My father was utterly disheartened to hear what conditions they had endured while building hundreds of barracks for an unknown purpose. The Germans, those cultivated people, did not supply food or water for their workers? Their forced labor. A people who for generations has defined itself as the most cultured people of Europe surely did not mistreat others? My father's theory began to crumble, and he was confused and incredulous. He began to doubt himself and lost confidence.

How could I expect my father to think differently? Everyone had similar views. The story from 1917 about General Ludendorff, the leader of the German war effort during World War I, was known. He spoke in Yiddish to the Jews of Poland and said "My dear Polish Jews..." Prior to what happened the optimists among us would say that the Germans were great, and still in 1938, it was hard to think otherwise and make people change their minds.

The day Hersh came home was the last day I saw my father smile. It was the summer of 1940 and no one could imagine the tragedy about to befall us.

As time passed, we started hearing strange rumors, stories of murders, executions, mistreatment and abuse of Jews in various places, but nothing was clearly defined yet. Jews were murdered without trials, without reason, sometimes by the Poles themselves. That created chaos within the community. If we could be "punished" and executed, perhaps we had reason to fear. In the meantime, the war was not ending. A few months had passed, and the relationship between Germany and Russia did not look fraught. They continued to trade, the Russians providing food, petrol and steel and in turn, the Germans sold them machinery and equipment. Fear was increasing among Jews and scary thoughts went through our heads.

It is worth noting that for a few months prior to the deportation from Sochaczew, a Jewish area had been delineated there. In 1940, it very quickly became a ghetto. On February 15, 1941, the ghetto in Sochaczew was closed, and we were deported to the Warsaw ghetto, which was not yet defined as a ghetto per se, but Jews could not reside beyond a clearly delineated area. As always with the Germans, everything was done secretly and through threats and warnings to the Judenrat. Any talk about what was going on would cause Judenrat members to lose their lives. This method was used in order to confuse and create chaos as well as to instill fear of the unknown. Thus, no one was able to plan anything with friends or family. The closing of the ghetto in Sochaczew gave the Germans the option to deport us to Warsaw ghetto and make the whole area West of Warsaw Judenrein – free of Jews. The area annexed to the Third Reich gave them an extra seven kilometers from Sochaczew, and that was their new border. By this time, we were forced to wear the Yellow Star.

The deportation was extremely hard for us. We lost our home and moved to an area where we knew few people and where we were forced to share an apartment with four or five other families. One of these families was my aunt and her children. We were not free to move about and could not leave the area. There were no means of survival, no way to support the family. Nonetheless, between February 15 and April 1, I managed to leave the ghetto at least twice.

Once I walked to Sochaczew, 50 kilometers away, to search for food. That was not an easy task since the ghetto was well guarded by Polish police in conjunction with Jewish police. All those who were caught with food were badly beaten. The food, usually a little bread or potatoes, would be confiscated. The police acted like servants of the Germans, inflicting pain on us before we even fell into German hands. But there was no other way to get food and we were all hungry.

The second time I left the ghetto, Hersh came with me. As we were walking, we had an ingenious idea, or so we thought. We were still utterly naïve and perceived the situation as if the world was normal. We did not know the show was run by a gang of murderers next to whom "regular" criminals were babies and the Mafioso a joke.

We decided to march to the Germans' Office of Labor, the Arbeitsamt, to describe to them what kind of conditions we and others were facing, thinking that they would surely understand our predicament. We would ask to work for food, not for money, and because we were from Sochaczew, we could also help them in return. That was our plan. How sadly naïve.

The Arbeitsamt was located across the street from the Gestapo. It was difficult to reach these offices as they were very heavily guarded by dozens and dozens of Germans. But we managed to pass through, and entered the office of the boss himself.

That day something happened to me that would repeat itself throughout the war, and that I cannot explain. Was it a miracle? I do not know. Maybe luck, whatever that is.

We asked to see the Head of the Office of Labor, and he immediately received us. That man had unlimited power and was authorized to do anything he wished. He proceeded to question us. Who we were, how we managed to leave the ghetto, it was so well guarded. We explained there was no food there, and that our family was hungry. Hunger opens every gate to a human being.

He immediately gave instructions to his associates and some food was brought in. He was incapable of understanding our story or our predicament. He called his deputy. They were incredulous that we had managed to leave the Warsaw ghetto and come to these offices. How could we have left when there were orders for us to stay put? How had we managed when the SS were ordered to guard and prevent escapes?

We answered all their questions meticulously and convinced them of the truthfulness of our account. They whispered to each other, were unsure about what decision to make, and invited us to sit down and finish our food and drinks. Finally, one of them said they would call on their neighbors the Gestapo across the street. We feared that the SS would be there in an instant to execute us. But then, almost simultaneously, the boss added he would not kill us because he did not want to give the SS the satisfaction, but that we had to leave using back roads. "Make sure you are not caught; make sure no one knows about your visit here; if anyone hears about this, they will kill you – and me – because I let you go. With time, you will be executed anyway, but at least I'll be spared as long as no one knows you were in this office."

Of course, we promised him everything. After a handshake and wishes for the best, we left this man, this angel who endangered his own life and did not call the SS, saving us from immediate death.

We rapidly left town. I was not to see it again until 1988.

We went back to our parents, brothers and sisters, who were worried sick about us. We returned to our fate. We gave them the food we had carried on the road, risking our lives to bring them nourishment. I will never forget that dear man in the Office of Labor to my dying day. He saved us. I do not know what he did later on, or where he was, but for years I dreamed about meeting him again. I do not even know his name, but he certainly should be listed as a righteous person. Of course, not many Germans, or others, behaved as he did, and that is a shame.

Starvation did not end after we had returned to the Warsaw ghetto. We still had to get food somehow. One way to do it was to leave the ghetto for various types of labor, or to barter, exchanging our clothing for food. That was easier said than done because of the searches performed at the gates.

At the beginning of April, with the cooperation of the Jewish police, the Germans began to round people up, especially youths, and taking them to unknown destinations.

It was then that Germans on motorcycles started shooting at people randomly. Hundreds of people were killed that way each and every day. It caused fear and panic and it was dangerous to be out in the street. The Germans also started closing off specific areas within the ghetto, searching for youngsters. Most of these maneuvers took place in the early hours of the morning when most people were asleep.

My mother knew what was going on. We could not protect her from the harsh reality. She would hear the shooting at night and understood what was happening. She was already very ill by then, weak and bedridden. One day, she asked that Hersh and I approach her bed. She turned to us and asked that we get organized to escape the ghetto without delay. Otherwise, she said, they would catch us, kill us, or send us somewhere. I must emphasize that at that point, we were not yet aware of the existence of concentration camps, death camps or labor camps. My mother said that this time we had to flee for good. We could not come back like the other times.

But we argued that Father could not, alone, take care of her and of the other children, and that we had to stay together. Mother said the only chance for us to stay alive was to leave. But how could we do such a thing at this difficult time? Mother's answer was loud and clear. Leaving would be our only chance of survival. "If both of you run," she said, "at least one of you will stay alive and live to see the end of the Germans and their conspirators." Neither of us could ever imagine that my mother's words would turn out to be the words of a prophet.

Forty-eight hours later, Hersh and I were ready to leave. We discussed our plans with Father and our siblings who did not understand what we were talking about. All they knew was that they were hungry and wanted to eat. "Bring us bread like before the war," they pleaded. They did not know, nor understand, that their two older brothers were leaving, never to return. Never would we bring bread again. Perhaps we would manage to stay alive, but at what price? This question remained unanswered as we were leaving the house in April 1941. We got up at four in the morning. I remember the time because we had planned it with Aaron Goldfarb, a childhood friend of mine. He was late, and we decided to wait for him no more than fifteen minutes. When he finally arrived, he informed us that the whole area was being closed in, and a round-up of youngsters – called Lapanka – was in progress. We needed to figure out how to reach the building of the Department of Justice at Przyogrodowa Street.

There was an alley called Leszno Street. One side of the pavement was situated inside the ghetto, the other was secured by Poles. How could we flee when the whole area was so heavily guarded? We quickly discussed our options with Father. There was no time for goodbyes. We were on the first floor, so we climbed onto a roof under one of the windows and jumped into the alley below. There was total silence. The guards were on the larger streets and near the ghetto gates. We advanced quickly and quietly until we reached a wooden wall guarded by a Jewish policeman. "You see," we told him, "there's three of us, and we're going to the Aryan side, and you're not noticing any of this. You never saw us." He looked at us, turned his back and moved away, pretending we were not there. We climbed onto each other's shoulders, jumped over the wall and fell directly into the hands of a Polish officer.

He was startled but offered to bring us a horse-drawn carriage if we bribed him. We did not argue, paid him off, and, in a few minutes, we were on our way from Warsaw. The carriage dropped us off at the edge of town. We started walking towards Radom. Our goal was the town of Ozarow Kielecki. It was far and we had to cross areas filled with hostile Poles and checkpoints manned by Germans. On the way, friends helped us with food and shelter. That was an incredibly difficult and dangerous undertaking.

In the mornings, we penetrated deep into wooded areas to sleep. We would walk at night. After a week, we arrived in Ozarow.

We wanted to go to a Krakow family we knew from Sochaczew. We thought that if they were still alive, and if Jews had not been ordered to leave, then perhaps we could stay with them until the end of the war. We felt we had no other choice. When we reached their house, rather a miserable shack but shelter nonetheless, we realized there was nothing for us to do there, except work for the Germans or die of hunger. There were the same restrictions for Jews there as everywhere else. Jewish areas were marked, and we could not cross them. The only difference was that the Jews here somehow managed to deal with the Poles. There were only two to three thousand people, with just a couple of hundreds of Jews. Thus, the possibilities were very limited, and it was hard to be in hiding without a means of survival.

We decided to look for work in neighboring areas. Many farmers needed help after the Germans had snatched most of their workforce. We could go to the villages and inquire; the Poles might agree to give us work despite the dangers they faced since they had no farmhands. We knew the deal. We would sleep in barns or pigsties, and in nice weather, we would sleep in the open fields. For our work, we would get food.

I stayed in the first village we found. Hersh stayed at a farm nearby, and Aaron found a place a little further down the road.

We were living relatively well. On Sundays, we would all meet in town, discuss current events and share our problems. We made some new friends, and we thought a lot about our future. Reality stood in stark contrast to our dreams and desires. We managed to stay in touch with our families in the ghetto and to send them food packages.

Through one of our contacts, I heard one day that my mother, who had been so ill and whom I desperately loved, was no longer alive. Hersh and I decided that he should go by train to Warsaw to bring Father and our siblings to where we were staying. Taking a train was a huge risk in itself, not to mention re-entering the ghetto and fleeing it again with Father and children in tow. It was a life and death gamble.

A week later, Hersh was back with Father and Bela, our seven-year-old sister. Father had not forgotten to bring with him his Tallit and Tefillin (Jewish prayer shawl and phylacteries used during prayer).

My other siblings had managed to flee from the ghetto and were wandering between the surrounding villages of Sochaczew. Perhaps they pretended to belong to groups destined for labor. Of course, this is pure speculation. There was no direct contact and much of what we knew was based on rumors. Until now I do not understand how Hersh managed to get Father and Bela out of the ghetto. It's not like we could bribe anyone – we had no means to do it. Still Hersh was successful, and I was glad they had joined us, although nothing was solved by their presence. We were still hungry and had a serious shortage of clothing.

The summer of 1941 arrived.

We felt uncertain and uneasy. We had high hopes that the Russians would perform miracles, but they bitterly faded when we heard about the developments on that front. It now seemed like the war would last longer than expected. Our situation was worsening, our hopes were crushed, and we were busy evading the Jewish police. We were outsiders in Ozarow, and we needed to be careful because the Germans routinely snatched youngsters for forced labor.

One day as I was resting after working on the farm, the farmer turned to me and asked if I'd be willing to convert to Christianity and marry his sister-in-law. The question scared me. I was surprised to hear such a strange request, and I knew I was unable to do what he asked. It was true, his sister-in-law was pretty, nice and healthy. But she was a villager with whom I had nothing in common. And I would not consider converting.

I postponed giving my answer through a number of excuses. I said I needed to think, to consult with Father and Hersh, and so on. Even this peasant knew what the outcome of a conversation with my father would be. "You're a Jew, but an intelligent one," he said to me. It was clear Father would never approve, although Hersh might, and my own opinion would not count for much.

I kept evading the subject every time the peasant brought it up until one day it was presented to me as an ultimatum. When I tried to dodge the question, he said the situation was worsening, and that if I did not marry her, I would have to leave. He would give me some food and perhaps something more, but I would have to leave. He added that he was taking a risk by having me work for him, and I understood the hint. In my utter naivety, I asked him how he would feel if I told the Germans that I had hidden in his house for eight months with his knowledge and consent. I said it half-jokingly, but before I had finished the last words of my sentence, I regretted what I was saying. I could not take the words back and I knew I had made a fatal mistake. There was no way back. I knew he could execute me at night when I slept. He could inform the Germans or the Polish police that he had killed a Jew and would receive some sugar, salt or vodka in addition to respect. I think he was so shocked by my impertinence and the fact I showed courage – what Jew spoke like that? – that he was literally speechless.

As for me, I could not correct my stupid, naive, terrible mistake. I immediately knew my life was not worth a cent. I had to flee. Still, I had dinner with the farmer and his wife as usual. In order not to arouse their suspicion, I proceeded to go to the barn afterwards to sleep.

That very night, I left the farm.

A heavy carpet of snow was covering the fields around me as I started to look for shelter. It was winter so the farms weren't really in need of workers. Still I went from farm to farm to look for work. I would sneak into barns and pigsties and after the farmers threw food for the pigs – usually potatoes cooked in their skins – I would gather it up and leave. It was dangerous to be seen wandering around, and the snow made my presence more discernable. For two weeks I looked for work until one day a peasant told me to go to the very edge of the forest, far from all the other villages. When I arrived there, I saw an isolated house. People might assume a forest guard was living there.

The man in that house was forlorn, like his house. He never ventured out or met with anyone and led a completely secluded life. He would go to church on Sundays, but he was anti-social and people thought him strange and ignored him. He had once attempted to become a priest but had failed his studies.

He was limping and needed help on the farm. A girl with a developmental handicap served as his slave, or Parobek, but she could not handle all the work. When the man heard I was from Sochaczew, he greeted me warmly and invited me inside. His seminary, where he had studied to be a priest, had been in Sochaczew, and I suppose for that reason we felt an immediate kinship. He said I should not fear the Germans, that they never came to such isolated places. He added that even the Poles stayed away and disliked him because he was a bachelor. The only person who would pass by was the forest guard. He told me I could stay with him. Did I have a choice? I did not.

What he considered good living conditions were not exactly paradise for me. As it turned out, my life took a turn for the worse. With time, I learned what the man's true intentions were. It was not that he wanted to save a Jew from the Germans, he actually admitted to being a fervent anti-Semite. He was glad to have me there just for the satisfaction of having a Jew slave away for him. It meant redemption, revenge on those he believed had killed his god. Even if he saved a Jew that was well worth it. I had to promise him that I would remain his slave even after the war ended. To make our arrangement final, he told me I had to marry that Parobek girl of his. That would strengthen his confidence regarding me, he argued. He was a priest, he could marry us, thereby forcing a Jew to convert to Christianity, a great achievement and a good deed in his eyes.

He truly treated me like a slave. I was not allowed to have warm water to wash myself, not that there was a shower. I was actually not allowed to heat water for any reason, even for washing clothes. His hatred consisted not of killing, but mistreating, abusing, torturing, humiliating and dehumanizing. I quickly understood that I had to flee this place too and look for a better home, regardless of the dangers I was running.

I had basically refused the two marriage proposals, one from a peasant, the other from a priest. Even then, at twenty years old, I knew more or less what alternatives I had in the outside world. I had no home. No one could help me. Logic dictated that marrying would be the simplest thing to do. But I could not imagine myself standing in front of a priest in a church with my name – as they suggested – changed to Wacek Brzozowski, my mother's maiden name. I could not stomach the idea of the cross above my head and the "sacred" water the priest would splash on me, thereby converting me to a Christian. I am not a religious person and I do not think any religion is superior to another, but a lot of suffering has happened throughout history to my people, the Jewish people, in the name of Christianity.

The idea of refusing or accepting a marriage proposal was not as easy or simple as it may seem today. I had to think quickly and make a decision then and there. Later, when I was in the camps, in the worst conditions ever endured by man, I often wondered about my decision and I regretted the choices I had made. I regretted not having the courage the make the right choice, the natural choice. I could have survived the war more easily. I know today, and I have no doubts, that I would not have been able to stand this test over time and face this lie within my soul. To stay true to my values, I preferred not to lie to myself and go to the unknown to prove to myself that I was a man of honor. Even today, with my many years of life experience, I would have made the same decision, sad as its outcome turned out to be.

The winter was nearing its end; the snow started to melt, and after a few days I found a place further along, a better place where a couple lived. They were peasants too. The man was ill and was unable to do any kind of work. The woman was a housewife. I worked for them in relatively good conditions. I also managed to help Father and Bela a bit more than previously. I would wake up as early as possible in the morning and did not stop working until nighttime. I put every effort into working well and working hard. The woman would mend my clothes and treated me very nicely. I did not know precisely where my siblings were, but I knew they had fled the ghetto, except for Rachel. After Father and Bela went to Ozarow, my sister Rachel, who was two years younger than me, stayed behind by herself.

For some reason, she was unable to flee the ghetto like Hersh and Father. I am sure Hersh did all he could to get her out of there, but she did not manage to join us. Even if she had been successful in fleeing the ghetto, her chance of survival would have been nil. But there, she stayed without parents, without siblings, with no family, and no one to care for her. How did she overcome these difficulties even for one day? I heard from a Sochaczew woman that she saw Rachel in the Umschlagplatz on her way to Auschwitz.

Two of my brothers, Haim and Jacob, and my sister Feige managed to escape from the ghetto to surrounding villages. There was no way for us to communicate, and we lived off rumors. That caused me great pain. I am not just speaking of the subhuman physical conditions, but of the emotional toll and pain, the longing, the unanswered questions, the fears, the doubts. Today I know that there was nothing we could have done differently, but it is hard for me to live with this tragedy in my heart. My family was destroyed by this "cultured" German people. I guess one can be barbaric and advanced at the same time.

One night, as the peasants and I were having dinner, a horse-drawn carriage stopped outside. A German and a Polish policeman, accompanied by the head of the village, Soltys, walked up to the farm.[1] They entered the house, except for the carriage driver. He told me he was angry at the Germans because they did not pay him for his labor. If I did not escape, they would take me to the local office and execute me there. I asked him to help me run away by cutting through the harness. I suggested that in order for him not to be blamed for my escape, he should let me run, then go inside the house and start screaming that I had fled, that I had a knife on me, that I had cut the harness, that he had seen nothing. It took some convincing, but he finally agreed. I jumped over the fence and ran towards the fields. He, in the meantime, proceeded to scream at the top of his lungs. I was more afraid of his screams than of the policeman because I thought the peasants would chase after me before they even understood what the matter was. Darkness was falling, and I was running. When the men came out of the house, I threw myself on the ground between rows of potatoes. They searched for a while, but unable to locate me they shot into the dark and left. Once again, I had been saved from certain death. Later that night, I returned to the couple. They were relieved and very happy to have me back.

As spring was approaching in the year of 1942, one day my little sister Bela showed up and told me that the Jewish police had caught and jailed Father. They demanded that my brother Hersh and I report immediately to the Judenrat, otherwise they would not let Father go. At night, Hersh and I went to see some friends we had made, and with their help, the police agreed to exchange one brother for Father.

Father was freed, and a discussion ensued as to who would replace him. Father seemed shocked, as if paralyzed, by this argument between Hersh and me. We assumed that going to a camp meant death, but still had no reliable information. We did know the Einsatzgruppen were killing Jews as they were approaching the Russian front. The Jewish police tried to calm us down by indicating that these were labor camps where people got food and shelter, but who believed them? The Germans had promised them certain things, but they were not reliable. There was no choice, however. One of us had to go. One of us had to report to the Judenrat the next morning. I was willing to go, anything to let my Father go free, and so was Hersh. We quarreled; I argued for my departure, Hersh for his. We were both ready to die to save Father, even though we knew he would not necessarily survive regardless. Finally, my case won favor. Hersh was taller and lighter than me, meaning he looked more Polish and could manage better among the Poles. He was also more experienced than me in life and would probably be able to help us more from the outside. Finally, he had been in the cavalry during his military service in the Polish army. He understood their mentality and language better and was more street smart. His chances of survival, we thought, were therefore higher.

With a bleeding heart, bitterness and sadness, we surrendered to my destiny of going to the camp. When we embraced to say goodbye, Hersh said to me: "I hope you will overcome the pain and suffering that you will meet, and that you will stay alive, and I hope that on the way back to the village, a stray bullet will hit my head and finish me off, so I won't have to live with all this pain."

It was April 1942.

As I was leaving, walking slowly towards the police, I looked back and saw Father cry. I never saw Father or Hersh again.

Later, when I was in the labor camp, I received some mail from them, and even a few food packages, but after a short time our connection was completely severed, and I stayed alone and lonely, longing for my family. I still miss them today, and I will miss them until the end of my life.

At that time, I could only guess what happened to them. One time, I dreamed that my sister Feige and two brothers Haim and Jacob were murdered in the very yard where I stood just before I was taken to the camp. It is possible. I am sure Father and Bela were sent to some camp, maybe Majdanek, and murdered there, like thousands of my people, like hundreds of thousands. Like millions. This is how a whole family was wiped out for no reason except that we were Jews. A whole family was murdered, and the world stood by in silence and watched. Perhaps the world was even satisfied, Germans were fulfilling everyone's secret desires.

The Poles certainly helped them as much as they could, and in return received a Jew-free country, Judenrein, a dream come true. We paid the price, everyone was murdering us despite hundreds of years of our struggle for an independent Poland, despite all the blood we had shed for this country throughout generations, despite hundreds of years of Jewish culture, theater, literature, music, journalism, science, medicine, and business and every type of constructive contribution to a healthy, vibrant society. All of this we had achieved in the face of virulent antisemitism fueled by the culture, church, schools, communities and society as a whole. The antisemitism in their bones made sure they did not hesitate in carrying out their new tasks in the roles of assassins.

When I recently visited Poland, I did not find the courage in my heart to go to that village and see if I could find out anything about the last days of my family members. When I discussed my dilemma with some Poles I knew, they suggested that if Poles had indeed murdered Feige, Haim and Jacob, then it could be dangerous for me to go there even though it was 1990.

April 1942 was a time when Jews were expelled from their homes, ghettos were closed and eliminated, and entire communities relocated. Simultaneously, the Germans started executing whole populations. This was also when labor camps for Jews who served the Germans, against their wills, by manufacturing equipment for war were created.

I arrived at the Judenrat, where two trucks were waiting. There were seventy of us. We were all young and from different places – only a handful were from Ozarow. Not one of us had any money whatsoever – those who did had bribed the Jewish police or the Judenrat and had been freed, saving themselves temporarily. We were double refugees, first from Sochaczew and then from Ozarow. Everyone, rich and poor, ended up in camps.

To my knowledge, most of the Ozarow Jewish population was sent to Majdanek. We all know what happened to them there. To date, I have never met a Jew who survived Majdanek.

Ukrainians accompanied us to the camp. They were wearing German uniforms and were still behaving nicely to us. After a few hours, we arrived at a camp named Skarzysko Kamienna. I had no clue what it was. I knew there was a city bearing that name in Poland, that was all.

When given the order, we got off the truck. We were told to assemble and walk towards the gate. The camp was situated between railroad tracks on one side and a three-meter concrete wall on the other side. It consisted of nine barracks and a tent for "showers", which were basically a pipe installed low like for a toddler with a number of faucets dispensing cold water only. That was where we were to wash and shave. Later we found out that there was a Jewish barber. We would give him some soup or a piece of bread or a rag, and he would shave us once a week or so. There was another awning built directly above a large hole: that was the latrine. We were informed what the order of each day was to be. We were to wake up at 5am, wash, shave and shine our shoes. No one knew how as there was nothing to do it with, no shoeshine tools of any kind. Then we would march to work while singing. These marches were organized by the Germans and intended to humiliate us.

At 7am we were to report to work, and we were not allowed to go near the fence. After listening to a long list of orders and regulations we had to follow, we were also informed that those who broke the rules would be executed.

Skarzysko Kamienna comprised three camps: Werk A, B and C. "My" factory, although located in Werk A – also known as "the small camp" – was recognized as the hardest and the worst. The majority of people died there. In Werk C, Jews were executed.

Skarzysko was owned, as were many other small camps, by HASAG, a large German armament firm. We were basically prisoners in a corporate-owned camp. Once inside the factory, Poles supervised the work and selected those who would work in the electric plant, known as Granatpresserei or Pociskownia in Polish. Poles supervised Jews selected to work in the electric plant, in transport and in the Granatpresserei.

I was in the last group along with a few other strong young men. We did not know what they would do with us, and we did not know that they would send us to what was known as the center of hell. That was the Lamaczka, where the labor consisted of working with steel, more specifically breaking steel posts. This department was part of the Granatpresserei. The work was extremely hard. Our clothes would get damaged, which was no small matter since there was no way to get other clothes. First, we transported pieces of steel to ovens, and after the initial processing, we took them outside. At that point, we still had no understanding of the equipment or way of carrying out specialized tasks.

This part of the factory was surrounded by equipment for steel cutting and on one side there were a few machines for sharpening saws. Next to it stood a machine for breaking square steel posts of 70mm by 70mm by 30cm in length; 100mm by 100mm; and 150mm by 150mm by 70cm in length. Later, these steel posts would go into machines at the Presserei that would make them round and ready for the bottle-shaped explosives. There were carts to move heavy equipment around in the middle of the factory.

Only Poles were working there when we arrived. Jews were not allowed to approach the machines. Another piece of equipment that we were not permitted to touch was a machine used to cut steel and produce spare parts. There were twenty machines in the factory, making an unbearable amount of noise. In addition, there were loud hydraulic machines.

Another department, adjacent to ours, had eight ovens. They were used to heat the steel we provided at 1,500 degrees Celsius. Two out of the eight could get to 1,800 degrees Celsius. Next to the ovens, there were immense machines of about 10 to 15 meters into which the steel would go to be flattened and formed. It was never cold in this part of the factory. We had to manufacture 5,000 to 7,000 pieces of artillery per shift. We were seventy young men, seventy hungry, tired, frail human beings working twelve-hour shifts around the clock. Those who worked at night "rested" during the day. Over time, not one Pole was allowed to use the equipment at the factory, except for three supervisors. One of them was overseeing the Polish department. I will write about him later.

It was clear to us that we would work in the harshest environment. We still did not know how bad it would become, that many people would die before we were freed. In comparison, the electric generator located across the department was considered paradise to work in, not because it was easy, but because there were only a few people there, and their relationship with the Poles was fairly good. Since they did not actually manufacture anything, there was minimal German supervision, and the Jews and Poles managed to do some bartering with food and clothing.

Because these were our first days there, we had to get up at 4am to get used to the rules, regulations and orders. We would also meet the camps' commander, Mr. Gnat, a Jew like us. The police also consisted of Jews; life in the camps was managed by Jews. The Germans came occasionally, in small groups, for the selections, to entertain themselves. We accepted what we heard at face value. We tried to behave well, like little children, and for now, we were hopeful that life would be bearable. The police told us that if we worked, we would get food, we would be able to rest at the end of the day and we would get clothing. Of course, we had no way of knowing what to expect, and what was really awaiting us. We had no idea what was going on in the small ghettos outside. Basically, we knew nothing, or close to it.

In her book *Death in Yellow,* Felicia Karai claims there is some disagreement as to the opening and closing dates of Skarzysko Kamienna. But I remember it well, because I was part of the initial group who arrived there, and I agree with Adam Rotkowski, whom she quotes. Unfortunately, I was also one of the camp's senior prisoners when it closed in the second half of 1944.

It was 4am and my first day in Skarzysko.

It was April 1942, a time well entrenched in my mind. The Jewish police burst into the barracks and woke us up with beatings, screaming and whistles. We ran around, semi asleep, not knowing exactly where to turn, where to go. Those who seemed a little lost got beat even more, and the chaos became uncontrollable. Half an hour later, there was total silence as we got some "coffee". The mixture consisted of water and some burned grain. As we had no cups, how were we supposed to swallow this mixture? We also got some jam. If someone asked about bread, they were told, "If you live by the end of the day, then maybe you'll get some bread." We were scared to hear this, but did not understand how to react. We had no spoons or forks and no plates. If we were to get lunch, how would we eat it?

The guards tried to calm us down, but they never stepped inside the factory, and did not have a clue either. It took us a few days to get organized enough to be able to get some food and a container to eat it from. The container was an old rusty can. We still needed a spoon. We were emphatically told that it was forbidden to have knives. If we were caught with something resembling a knife, we would be executed.

We had to stand in formation again, only to be told one more time what the rules were. The list of Dos and Don'ts was related by Gnat, a young man of twenty to twenty-five years old. He was flanked by Werkschutz personnel, the Ukrainians who were guarding the factory. Then, Almighty Gnat ordered us to march in groups of three. Each time we stood in military formation, they counted us at least once, more often twice or three times, until their numbers matched. We had to stand to attention with our hats off. Every time we walked through the gate, we marched in formation and were counted. Every time we marched to and from the factory, we had to sing. We sang, we cried, we did not know where we were going. It took two hours to get back to the barracks after endless formations and counting and standing to attention.

Following a night shift, it would be 10am before anyone laid down to rest. If someone got up, no one else could sleep. At 11am, someone had to bring "lunch". There was always a volunteer to bring it, but it made it impossible to sleep for those of us who had worked the night shift.

The steel factory took many lives, more than any other factory in Werk A and maybe more than in Werk C. The problem was not just the Werkschutz and the German supervisors. When the Germans started sinking into the Russian mud, and needed more artillery, bombs, spare parts and other equipment, under pressure from the German military command, and because of the lack of Polish manpower, we were required to perform more complicated tasks such as the cutting of steel using machines. My friend Leon Goldbaum was supposed to work on a huge steel-cutting machine, and I was transferred to another factory called Butelkownia where we changed the 150mm shell into something resembling a bottle, which gave the factory its name. I stood in front of two ovens with a total of six holes of 25cm in diameter. I had to carry a 70kg shell and throw it inside the hole. If I missed, it could fall and break my legs. One could not survive in a camp if one was injured, especially as a Jew. The Poles would have hit me. I quickly learned how to do the maneuver with the shells, and the Polish supervisor told the German head of the factory that I excelled at my work. What a miracle that was – a Jew who could excel at such complicated and hard work.

Therefore, they officially declared that Scheinwald was not a Jew. "He not only knows how to work hard, but he also eats pork," they decreed. A Jew was incapable of that in their eyes.

With time, they started giving us more advanced tasks, such as steel cutting on sawing machines and welding work. When I started working there, there were two or three other ovens. A Pole was working on one oven on one side, and I replaced another Pole on a trial basis.

The Poles ended up helping me by giving me the food they refused to eat. Sometimes the Polish supervisor even gave me food from his home, including pork. The Poles lived in their own houses and brought their own food. Food would be brought in for them, but they would refuse it because it was so bad. Still, our food was worse, and they would trade us their portions. They would get paid very little and were unable to make deals on the black market.

Two weeks after I started working there, a delegation of Germans, including German military officials, came to the factory. The Polish supervisor, who wanted to flaunt his talents, specifically how he had taught a Jew to work, brought them near the ovens and ordered me to show them what I could do. I executed my task perfectly, but I noticed some dissatisfaction on their faces. They walked away and whispered something among themselves. Then they called the head of the department and he ordered me to return to the Granatpresserei. As a "reward", I was to cut 150mm steel posts.

When the Poles worked there, the quota was 120 pieces per shift. Jews had to produce 180 pieces. That was difficult. Nonetheless, I overcame the difficulties and did my work properly. My friends also did well, and with time, we learned how to slow the machines down, and make it look as if the machines could not manufacture that many pieces per shift. They brought in some Germans who checked the machines and said they could produce 350 pieces every twelve hours. We had no choice but to perform. One must remember that each piece weighed 70 kilograms – 155 pounds. Our own weight was half of that for lack of nutrition.

We made a few attempts at sabotage, which was extremely dangerous. We intentionally broke some saws, then claimed the steel was not uniform, that it was too soft, or too hard, and thus the machines would break. We had to be very careful so that we would not be caught or blamed, but rather the equipment or the raw material seen as the culprits. If anyone was caught, he would be executed, no questions asked.

Across from "my" factory, near the electric generator, there was a department called Laznia. This was where all the transports arrived. The people were sent to the showers which served as the primary meeting place. We always wanted to know if someone, anyone, had heard about our families, get fresh information, or even rumors, and meet old friends and acquaintances. We lived with the hope of good news, but I never heard anything about the people I cared about and loved.

One day, as I was working, I heard noises coming from the direction of the showers. I went outside to look and saw a new transport of Jews. Just before I left the factory, I noticed that Leon was not in front of the machine with which he was supposed to cut steel. I noticed a large steel post turning freely on the machine with oil pouring down from it. I walked away quickly so that I would not be blamed for sabotage and went to look for Leon. He, in the meantime, was looking for someone in the transport to give him news. I told him what had happened with the machine and we both agreed to tell the Polish supervisor. When the Pole realized what had happened, he did not know what to do, and called the German supervisor Karel Proccher.

Proccher arrived in his usual blue gown, put his head in his hands and said "sabotage". That meant the death penalty for Leon. The Polish supervisor pointed at Leon, who was immediately slapped on the face. "Why did you do this?" he asked. Leon explained that he had not done anything, that it had just happened, that the machine was not functioning properly. With my testimony, the man calmed down a bit and started talking to himself. "How can we resolve this?" he mumbled to himself. Later the machine was taken out and exchanged for another. As a punishment, Leon was placed in front of one of the ovens and had to move shells inside to cool down. The temperature of these shells reached 800 degrees Celsius. After he had worked there for a while, he was put back on the original machine he had been assigned to.

I have no idea how the German managed to explain the failure of Leon's machine. I do not know why they did not investigate or punish Leon. In any event, nothing happened, and Leon continued to work as before, and the subject was closed. There were no guards per se in the department, just one Polish supervisor. We had to meet our quotas. Sometimes we would claim we had fewer pieces than we actually had. It took a while before the steel was cut, so we had a couple of minutes without activity. We could leave the area and head to the showers. The Poles did not care that we were walking around, they just wanted the ovens to be full. For example, Leon would get a large piece of steel and wait until it was ready for use, that is, break from its original one meter in diameter. That process took about half an hour, so Leon was free to leave for that time. Later on, I learned that he enjoyed some "privileges" which helped him survive. From the end of the war until his death Leon lived in Haifa.

We were allowed to wash once in a fortnight. I could wash more often because my department was close to the showers. If it was feasible, I would wash once a week using warm water and soap. During the wash, my clothes would be disinfected, and I did not suffer from lice. Most people had to endure lice because they were not allowed to come to the showers. Some washed once every month or even once every two months. They would wash in the camp under short pipes with cold water. In the summer it was more bearable, but in the winter, the pipes would freeze and crack. One problem men faced was shaving. We were not allowed, nor did we have, any shaving tools – they clearly represented a great threat to the Reich and were thus forbidden. But we had to be clean-shaven and have shiny shoes. Otherwise, we ran the risk of being executed. There was a barber as I have mentioned, where it was easier to stand in line during the night shift, but it always cost a vegetable, a piece of bread or a quarter of a cigarette. Without giving something up, it was hard to get shaven. Shoe shining was mandatory but impossible to accomplish. We had to find a way to have our shoes shined if we wanted to live.

No one dreamed of washing clothing. That was impossible. We could only get them disinfected, which was a task in itself. Generally, the workers in one department lived in the same barrack, and it allowed my friends and me to keep ourselves cleaner.

There was a toilet in the camp. It was a hole in the ground framed by a round structure with a suspended wooden floor above it. We would stand in endless lines to use this toilet. Women had similar toilets to the men. We spent a large part of our miserable lives in line for the toilets. Most of us suffered from dysentery because of the rotten food. We were afraid of selections, and from fear, we could not finish what we needed to do in the toilet, because there was a lot of pressure from the line, and the police would rush us, and people would get sick. Almost all aspects of camp life could be observed in this line – trading, bartering, stories told about home, stories of unrequited loves, the longing for friends and family, contagious weeping, people fainting from exhaustion. Many did not need the toilet anymore by the time they got there. Suffering from dysentery, they could not control themselves, and often they fell down and died. This was true in every camp. In many camps there was even a toilet supervisor, Scheissmeister or Scheisskapo. He was responsible for the toilets and what went on near or around them.

A few words about clothing in Skarzysko: it was a camp that was different from others in this respect, because sometimes they changed our clothing. The frequency of that happening depended on their mood, and it did not happen too often, only when the clothing was totally threadbare and only if we "deserved" it. More often than not, they would select a person by how tatty his clothing looked and execute him. That way was more effective and cheaper.

More transports would arrive. There were people who had lived in the ghettos, as the ghettos had now been liquidated. The new transports brought young people, stronger and healthier than we were. The great majority of us were lonely, without any family. Sometimes a son and father would arrive together, but that was rare. We would hear more and more horror stories about the transferring of Jews to unknown places. We tried to learn more, and desperately searched for familiar faces. It was through the new people that we received information about what was going on outside our prison camp, including at the front. Most new people had to join in the terrible burden of the harsh work. There was unspeakable suffering, hunger and selections that would break the newcomers who fell like flies. Most of them ended up in the forest in Werk C, where death units took care of them. The assassination units consisted of Germans and Ukrainians.

In Werk A there were 3,000 to 5,000 people maximum. In Werk B there was about 1,000 people and Werk C had about 2,000. Altogether, there were never more than 10,000 people in the whole camp at any one time.

While the Germans did not get involved in everyday life in the camp and the factory, they would sometimes enter the compounds to do selections. The Gestapo did not fully control Skarzysko, nor other camps that HASAG owned. HASAG dictated how things were run and made most of the decisions based on their own interests. We now know that HASAG decided not to destroy the camp against the wishes of the SS and the Gestapo. HASAG proved to Hitler that they were the largest producer of weapons to the Germans on the Russian front – they were also located the closest – and from the highest ranks of the government it was decided with HASAG not to destroy the camp. Instead, they decided to move the inmates to a death camp, close the factory but leave the buildings. So the camps were left standing, and they brought in populations from the ghettos and from Majdanek, Auschwitz and Plazow. HASAG was interested in keeping the buildings intact, the people were irrelevant for them.

In other words, HASAG had more clout and political power than the SS and the Gestapo. They made money by exploiting us as slave labor. They had an economic interest in free manpower, pure and simple. They kept us in sub-human conditions. A lifespan in Skarzysko was generally no longer than one week. The same went for Schlieben, another HASAG camp. In Schlieben, the Gestapo murdered people and HASAG did not care at all. By July-August 1944, there were no more death camps on Polish soil; the camps had been destroyed. Thus, they had no means to systematically annihilate Jews. They had too many people, so they killed us. HASAG let the Gestapo do as they pleased. Some of the food that we were supposed to receive was stolen, some even by the Gestapo.

In a way, there were conflicting interests: kill the Jews or continue production as cheaply as possible and maximize profit. The economic factors were overshadowed only by the fact that the Germans running HASAG were cooperating with the regime and wanted us dead. If HASAG were ever concerned about our living conditions, we never knew about it. The Jewish police controlled everything within the compound of the camp itself. They followed instructions from the few Gestapo officials that were present.

Once the Germans decided to hold a selection, they would bring in a large force of Ukrainians, the Werkschutz, who surrounded the camp, heavily armed with automatic weapons, and killed according to orders issued by the Germans. A small group of armed Germans would then enter the camp. We were ordered to stand to attention in the assembly area. There were four assemblies of three rows, each row forming a square around Appellplatz. Then the Germans would indicate to the Jewish police how they wanted the selection to be conducted. They would take out a whole row, each third person in a row, the middle row, each two lines, whatever they felt like on that day. The "chosen" ones would then march to the left, or right, surrounded by Germans and Ukrainians, and taken out of the camp to Werk C, where the Ukrainians executed them. The reason for the number of armed murderers guarding us during selections was that they were afraid there would be unrest, so they were prepared to assassinate us if needed. We would run around like mice before each selection, trying to figure out where to place ourselves so we would not be designated for death that day, as if we could predict how the Germans would do the selection. They were completely arbitrary. Each time, the Germans found new, inventive ways to keep things entertaining for them and confusing for us. We tried to guess what type of selection would be made on a particular day and shuffle ourselves into order accordingly.

Selections in the Lazaret, the "clinic" or infirmary, were run by the Jewish police once every two weeks. The Jewish police, while not armed with weapons, did carry sticks. Accompanied by a German (who would not actually enter the "clinic" for fear of contracting our diseases), they would perform the selection by picking on the sick and the weak. There, people had no strength to resist, and mostly remained passive. Only in a few instances did anyone argue with them. A Ukrainian or two would lead these poor souls into the forest.

Often selections were held in the factory itself. The Germans killers took their job seriously but chose people lightly without the help of the police. They would catch us right before we would take up our positions in the factory – each department heading for their respective equipment –take out a certain percentage of the men, lead them out of the factory and accompany them to Werk C. The Germans were careful not to get lice or diseases from us and were therefore happy not to enter the camp, but that did not stop them from occasionally murdering 50 people, or 100 people, just for sport. Selections constantly took place in the camp and during work. Even those in excellent physical condition went through selections. Those the Germans missed once were not missed again. As more selections were taking place, masses of new people would arrive; there was always the same number of slaves, the level remained constant even though new transports unloaded their human cargo.

In Werk C they filled shells with various types of gunpowder, especially picric acid and Trotyl, an explosive powder. People would turn yellow from these products, and the dust would penetrate every orifice in their bodies and through their skin, destroying their frail health. When the Poles were working there, they used gas masks and special protective clothing, and had better food and milk to help them cope with these dangerous powders. But the story was different for Jews. Their hair went yellow and would often fall out. People were weakened and would collapse and die in the middle of their work.

Those, who despite these conditions, managed to survive never made it past the selections in Skarzysko. German and Ukrainian assassins murdered the yellow people. Thousands were killed in Werk C; we knew what was going on there. Like all other Skarzysko prisoners, they were allowed to shower once every two weeks. We would learn what was happening from them then.

One day, a group from Werk C came to shower, and I wandered around looking for a familiar face. Suddenly, I heard my name. I turned around and saw a man older than me call me by my name. It was an old neighbor, Yeoshua Zavadezki, or Joszua Zawadzki in Polish. He was unrecognizable. He told me there were three others in that group from my hometown. I met them later and tried to help them as much as I could, which was very little. We would speak about our homes, and every time we split, we cried. Two of these people, Yechiel Zand and a woman whose last name was Cohen, stayed alive.

We lived off rumors. We also read bits and pieces in newspapers that the Germans threw away. We could not put our hopes in the partisans. There was no chance that they would help us because of the camp's location, which was in a heavily populated and industrial area. The only chance would be to try to get help from Poles if we managed to escape. But that did not happen. Although the population was socialist, they were (and still are) anti-Semitic. After the war, pogroms against Polish Jews who returned to Poland were orchestrated by Polish groups, and Polish individuals murdered Jews who dared go back to search for their home or property. For example, in Kielce, a town near Skarzysko, twenty Jews were murdered after they managed to survive the war. Those who wanted to flee had no chance, so we stayed with our dreams and faced our days hoping we would overcome our plight.

In the middle of 1943, after the defeat of the Germans near Stalingrad and in Africa, we started hearing about what was going on at the fronts, and we heard rumors about partisans fighting. We also heard from the Germans themselves. Many Poles told us with pride that "their" Jews were fighters. No one told us that some of their Polish heroes also fought the Jews, thereby helping the Germans and undermining their own positions. It was important for them to finish their deals with Polish Jews and receive from the Germans a Poland free of Jews, which they did. I want to relate part of a story that appeared in the *Sochaczew Journal*, pp. 514-532:

'*A young man managed to go to Eastern Poland to organize a small group of young Jews. Somehow they managed to get weapons and flee into the forests to start a partisan group who fought the Germans and joined the Bilski unit. Under the leadership of this Bilski, a Jew, 1,500 Jews – young, old, women, children and a few fighters – joined the group. One day, a group left to do some work in a village, and there they met Polish partisans. The Poles invited them into a house, gave them food and water, and immediately afterwards forced them to put their arms down. At night they executed them. One of the members was Istche Berel from Robaswicz. He arrived at the partisans' headquarters and told them what happened. The news was transferred to Moscow and from there an order came to take away the Poles' weapons. There were large Jewish partisan groups who could confront these people, and they were eliminated promptly. In many places where partisan Poles encountered Jews, they would murder them. But this was the first time partisan Jews eliminated partisan Poles.'*

The transports kept coming and the murderers kept murdering and every day more people were missing from the factory and new people arrived. The responsible German parties made sure of this. Thus the number of people in the camp remained constant. In the meantime, we arrived at the factory gate at 6.30am, and after assembly work started at 7am. The number in the formations was smaller. We changed over with the night shift and worked incessantly until 7pm. Then another assembly, change of shift and march to the barracks.

At 12.30pm there was a brief break. Someone brought an aluminum barrel with 60 liters of "food" and a smaller one with additional "food". During the night shift, the break was at midnight, and generally the food was thicker and the portions larger. This was one of the reasons we preferred to work at night. We gauged the value of the "soup" by placing a spoon vertically in it. Depending on how rapidly the spoon tilted and fell back into the liquid, we would decide what to barter for it. If the spoon fell immediately, the soup had very little bartering value. Sometimes we managed to get more food by bartering with the Poles. At night, it was also easier to send someone to look for food or buy it from another department. That person would bring it back and we would share it; it gave us a little strength to keep on living and working. We would invent so much nonsense to help us exist physically that no one would come up with under normal circumstances. Those who were not creative enough, those who could not find new ways of survival, were gone. They would be chosen in selections and taken to Werk C to be executed.

Food was, of course, critical. The Germans knew it and made sure there was no contact between us and the kitchen. In Skarzysko, the kitchen was in Werk A, in the factory area. But it was not a kitchen as we know it today. There were no dishes, and Jews were not allowed to work there. It was even forbidden for Jews to enter that area. Food was cooked there for all the factory workers, including the Poles and the few Germans and Ukrainians who agreed to eat in the camp. They had their own dining room, and the Poles would receive their barrels in their respective departments. The food first went to the Germans and Ukrainians and all those in uniform. Then the Poles would get their food, which was often so bad that they traded it with us.

We received the worst parts. A rotten piece of meat would be given to us, and even that rotten piece of meat was rare. Mostly, we received any vegetable that had been previously thrown in the garbage, like rotten cabbage. Sometimes they mixed in dehydrated potato flakes, which had zero nutritional value. Most of our so-called soup consisted of a liter of this watery liquid, plus 150 to 200 grams (5-7 ounces) of potato-based bread. Very seldom did we receive some spoiled sausage that the Poles and others refused to eat.

Food distribution was methodical, abiding to German order. The line was silent and no one pushed although we were all starved. If someone dared to move, he risked his life by doing so. He was beaten to death, killed by Germans or Ukrainians. I can testify to countless such murders. The Germans issued orders and we had to follow them. There was no flexibility unless we wanted to die. We were hungry, but the food could not sustain us and was not fit for human consumption. For the Germans, order was of the utmost importance. Many died standing in line. The barrels were large and sometimes when the Germans got mad, they would throw a Pole inside a barrel and seal it.

I managed to keep on going without clothes, without shoes, or without soles on my shoes. It was very hard to hide anything from the Jewish police, the camp being so small, just nine barracks, and almost everyone knew everyone else.

One day I was told by one of the guards that I had to bring the barrels of food to the factory along with a small group of other people. As a reward for this extra work, it was customary that we would get the leftovers at the bottom of the barrel. The Polish guard then ordered me to bring the barrels back. That was unusual. I was working the night shift, so I told the policeman, "This is not the usual procedure, I must get back to the Granatpresserei." He thought for a minute and then started beating me with a thin stick until my whole back was slashed. I asked him why he was doing this to me. He responded that I did not do what he, a policeman, had told me, and that he would beat me until I died. Later I understood that he had spotted that Gnat, the camp commander, was making his rounds. He had also seen the camp's big boss, a Gestapo man in his black uniform, and that was enough for him to show off how hard he could beat me and how efficient he was. He hurt me so badly, I could not bear it anymore. I ran towards the Nazi screaming, "Please kill me!" The Nazi took out his stick and hit me some more. He hit me on the head, and as he was beating me, he started kicking me with his boots. Before I fainted, I could hear him say, "You will die anyway, it's a pity to waste a bullet on a miserable creature like you."

That same Polish policeman who had beaten me so badly was later sent to a camp called Schlieben in Germany. I met him there, doing labor. He was like us then, a sad and emaciated slave, what we called a "Muselmann".[2] When he saw me, he turned to me and asked if I remembered who he was and what he had done to me two years prior in Skarzysko. He also asked me to give him food. Of course I remembered who he was, and if I had known how, and could have, I would have helped someone else instead. He was unable to stand on his feet and before the end of the night shift, he was dead. I tell this story with some degree of satisfaction, but not with revenge in my heart.

Conditions were bad for all of us, and I never felt any desire for revenge against some miserable Polish policeman who was not too smart. I still did not know well the Jewish police and their commanders, Tepperman and Krzepicky, whom I will mention later. This episode was one of many similar situations that happened to me – to us – in this cursed camp called Skarzysko Kamienna, Werk A.

After three to four months spent in the small camp, we were ordered to dismantle the barracks because we were moving elsewhere. Of course, there was no time for any questions and no one could provide trustworthy answers, but the rumor was that we were moving closer to the factory's gate. We hoped to rid ourselves of the Werkschutz, who always accompanied us to work, and dared to hope the marching and singing would stop. In a short time, we were transferred to a building named Ekonomia within the camp. We would see it on our march to work, but I did not and still do not know what purpose it had previously served. That building housed about 2,000 people. It was well built. There were huge halls inside, and along the walls, there were three levels of wooden boards to serve as beds. There was crumbled straw to sleep on but minimal space.

In comparison, in Werk A, we had two levels of boards and separate boards for people. We still had bedbugs and lice, but now everything became very crowded. It was impossible to rest after the work shift. That was very dangerous because people could not stand on their feet and work when they had had no rest whatsoever. We were at a critical stage. The rotation of people increased. Transports kept arriving. They had many to choose from during selections, and as people weakened because of a lack of rest and food and continuous hard labor, selections were held more frequently, and it was becoming dangerous even for those whose physical condition was relatively good.

At the same time, the pressure in the factory intensified as the Nazis were marching into Russia. It was unclear to us how the Red Army was so ineffective in tackling the German military machine. We thought the Red Army was big and great and could fight the whole world and win. We needed a Russian victory so badly that we forgot how in 1939 when I first arrived in Bialystok and saw Russian soldiers, I was overcome with excitement, and imagined in my young state that only they could be victorious in war.

The Red Army had beautiful march music, their singing was

impressive, and their horses and cavalry unequalled in grace, so I thought. We did not know that they lacked weapons, that their guns were strapped onto their shoulders with rope, and that often their long coats – Shinel – were held together with string. Their shoes, contrary to what we had imagined, were often rags. The Polish military had nice shoes – we know how much that helped them. They knew how to march properly and parade, but when it came to fighting, they lost their homeland in seventeen days. Maybe the Russian way was right, and in comparison, maybe their military might was superior to the Poles'. We still wondered when we saw men marching alongside carts and horses, many and large divisions walking long distances.

Additionally, we did not comprehend how a country as large and strong as Russia could not overcome a tiny country like Finland, where they were experiencing military defeats. These were unanswered questions. We continued to manufacture weapons for the Germans who we hated at least as much as they hated us, and we had no choice but continue to do hard labor, because we were prisoners and slaves. We were manufacturing ammunition for our enemy to use against those we hoped would free us. At the same time, if we were not productive, the Germans would have no reason to keep us alive and would eliminate us. They did so regardless. We were living this paradox, if you could call it living. All we did was wait for a miracle to happen but it never did.

The elimination the Jews continued relentlessly, and the world knew about it and ignored matters, waiting for the Germans to solve what they defined as the Jewish problem. How was this possible? Did everyone become a Nazi?

The Poles want a Judenrein or Polska Bez Zydow – Poland free of Jews – a term they learned from the Germans. The Russians were not too sorry about our fate either, there was nothing the Ukrainians would not do for the Germans, and in all of conquered Europe, there were collaborators who helped them. Where was America the Great and the Wealthy which, alone, could act but did nothing? After the war everyone would say that they spared no effort to help us, to free us from hell, and relate how many soldiers gave their lives to save us; in the meantime, we remained victims of mass murder. No one wanted us. Even if someone managed to escape from the camp, and was discovered by Poles, they would identify the person as a Yid. Often, they themselves executed Jews, or handed them to the Germans for a bottle of vodka or a kilogram of sugar. In this atmosphere we worked and it was immensely difficult.

One day a truck arrived with machinery. All the equipment was promptly replaced in the factory; the new machines worked faster and made it even harder to keep up. We had to adapt to a new rhythm. Living conditions did not improve. "Coffee" in the morning, some foul liquid called soup at lunch, and about 150 to 200 grams of bread in the evening. They demanded more arms and ammunitions and beat us more than ever. The Ekonomia building was so crowded that both the day and night shift slept on the same boards and never-replaced straw.

One morning, I stood at assembly before marching to work. Just before, I had managed to get a piece of bread, and I tried to eat it, but I could not because the bread tasted bitter. I quickly realized that I was sick. I went to work anyway but was incapable of standing up. Somehow I managed to make it through the day with my friends' help, and I returned to the camp. By then, I could not even eat and I was burning up with fever. It was a very serious situation. The next day, I could not get up and I had no choice but go to the Lazaret. A Jewish doctor was there, and a nurse who "treated" the sick. Dr. Sacks, Mr. Finger, an assistant and his wife Lola. They had no medication, no bandages, and worse, no desire or inclination to help. That I knew even before I went there, but was no alternative. I knew that no one came out of there alive, but I was dizzy with fever.

Inside, I was directed to a specific area. There was straw covered in lice and bugs, the same as was used for all prisoners. I lay down and lost consciousness. At noon, there was "food", but only for those able to get up on their feet and go take it themselves. Those unable to stand up would be even weaker the next day, and in two days' time they would lie on a cart outside, taken to the forest to be shot. I could not get up.

One of the people who worked at the electric generator was Moshe Wallerstein (Mosze Walersztein in Polish). He had arrived from Warsaw on a transport similar to mine. He took a liking to me, maybe because I had also come from the Warsaw ghetto. It was nice to have someone who cared about me, who could sometimes help to the best of their ability. I was lucky to have him as a true friend. He had a knack for maintaining a good relationship with the Poles and managed to trade with them. His greatest dream was that after the war he and I would move to Australia and become millionaires. To reach that point, we needed to be alive. He was ready to do anything to help me survive. In this place, that was no easy task. It was rare to get any help, especially from someone who was a complete stranger. All we had in common was that we both came from Warsaw ghetto, and that we had managed to escape the ghetto inferno and move to a greater hell. This man, with an iron will, managed to barter with the Poles and thus helped me leave the Lazaret, that death factory, alive.

He would bring me rolls and milk every day, even when I was

unconscious. These were unbelievable wares, a very rare treat in those days. He risked his life not just by showing up at the infirmary, but also by walking near people sick with typhus, like myself. He did not leave my side until I ate the bread and drank the milk. The doctor and nurse could not care less. They were sitting in some shack that served as an office, away from the sick. No one wanted to enter the premises because of the risk of contagion. When one day Wallerstein was caught entering the barrack with the rolls and milk, he was thrown out, and someone stole the precious bread and milk from me as I lay unconscious. That was a death sentence. But Moshe Wallerstein was not one to give up and kept coming with bread and water and waited until I was finished eating. He was ready to take a chance to save me. Instead of sleeping, he would sit by my side, but he could not stay long. I had to swallow the food quickly before he was thrown out. After ten days, with his encouragement, I managed to get up from the "bed" and got ready to stand in formation in front of my kings, the almighty murderers, as they were preparing to make their selections.

The Germans never entered these barracks, and Dr. Sacks, Moshe Finger and Lola were responsible – under Gnat's supervision – for the selections. By then Gnat was The Authority in the camp even though he was no longer the camp's commander.

They could decide if I lived or died, if I continued to work or was killed, and even the Germans accepted their decision without fail. It was known that those selected were led to the forest and executed. The rest of us would be assassinated at a later date. I presented myself to Sacks as I was ordered and begged to be spared. I was told to run along the barrack and back, which I could not do. Somehow, I managed to drag myself to the other end of the barrack and come back, like a drunkard. The doctor told me to go to the cart since I could barely stand on my feet. I attempted to explain to him that I was a veteran, an old-timer at the camp, a senior who had arrived with the first group, and the only one who remained alive from that initial set of seventy young human beings. Mrs. Lola slapped me so forcefully that I fell to the floor and could not get up. At that moment Gnat turned to the doctor and ordered him to release me.

"It is true," said Gnat, "we should keep the seniors. I've known Scheinwald since he first arrived at the camp. He's a good guy."

They decided that I was free to live for a little longer; Lola was really unhappy about it. Gnat called a policeman to accompany me back to my group of workers. I was lucky again that my group was working the night shift, and I immediately joined them and went to work. Once there, my friends helped me with food and rest and I managed to recover. That was not easy either, and Moshe supported me until I could help myself again.

At the end of the week, our night shift ended, and Monday morning after assembly, we marched to work again. We noticed that something was different. There were too many Germans and Ukrainians, and we heard a lot of screams. We had just started the shift when the Germans broke into the department and started selecting the weak to take outside, me included. Twelve people were brought out. A Ukrainian Werkschutz guarded us until everyone that had been selected was outside. Our backs faced the factory and our faces were turned to the gate.

Suddenly I felt someone kicking and hitting me. I turned and saw the Polish head of the department yelling at me: how had I managed to leave my post in the factory, I was committing sabotage. He ordered me to return to work immediately, otherwise they would kill me. He kept screaming that the department was not operating, that my machine was idle, and that there was no one to cut the steel and feed it to the ovens. The Ukrainians were startled, but he was adamant that he could not let me go. One Ukrainian then said he needed twelve men to give to the Germans, but if the Pole was willing to exchange me for someone else, he did not care, as long as he had twelve men. The department supervisor promised him someone else. I was "freed" and ordered to return to my post.[3]

They terminated their selection having chosen a number of people representing 15% of the Jewish labor force, seventy people, at the factory. They were led to Werk C and executed. After we returned to the camp later that day, we were saddened to learn that they had carried out a selection there too and taken 15% of the Jews to be assassinated. That day, at least 600 human beings were selected from Werk A. I read different numbers in different books, mostly based on Polish estimates and Gestapo data from HASAG. There is no doubt in my mind that these are not reliable sources, and that it is in their interest to minimize the death toll. Their numbers do not reflect the reality we experienced.

The Polish archives' statistics for Werk A, B and C are false, and they are covering up not only for themselves, but Poles in general as well, by saying people escaped or were given by the AK, Armja Krajowa. The Poles did not and still do not want the world to know the extent of what took place in these camps. Of course, they had no interest in HASAG knowing the exact number of people murdered and thus they decreased the true number. We, the camp's prisoners, knew the truth. We knew it even while we were in the camp. We are the true and only witnesses. We were the slaves; we saw the murders happen every single day and every night for thirty months. We do not need archives, or back-ups, or doubtful testimonies. In one way or another, during those thirty months at least eighty people, mostly Jews, were assassinated in Skarzysko every day. A very small number of the dead were Poles. Masses of people died of "natural causes", that is, starvation and disease. Those are not counted in the statistics. It does not matter how people died or from what – bullets, starvation, typhus, desperation. Everyone was murdered. What I described was just one arbitrary selection, but there were many, many selections like that one.

After each selection, there was a lack of manpower but there were no more people in the ghettos. Still, the Germans needed ammunition for their war. A large part of the goods did not make it past the borders because the partisans destroyed it on the way, bombing trains, so we needed to produce more and more. The Germans needed us to manufacture armaments, so they needed the manpower. But the manpower was basically Jewish, so we thought we had a chance to survive until the war was over.

One day, the Germans decided to bring in Jews from Majdanek. There was a man there named Silver who came from Sochaczew and had organized a partisan group. He was a young tailor who had fled from the ghetto. Those who lived on the Eastern side of Poland could reach the forests and become partisans. There were cases of whole families who lived in the forests within and among partisan groups. Partisans would attack the Germans, bomb police stations and trains etc., and caused damage beyond the Russian front. Jews fought for their lives against the Germans and the AK (the AL, Armja Ludowa, the army of the people, received support from the Communists).

One night, during the night shift, something happened with the senior Polish supervisor. He was not known as a Jew lover, but I had a very decent relationship with him. He had saved me once from selection, and during that night shift, he saved me again. It was Saturday night, the end of the Shabbat, and there was no shift after us. Usually we worked seven days a week, except in this case, and sometimes we got a day off for New Year, for example. We needed to clean the machines and the department and turn off the lights. After I finished cleaning, I pulled at the lamp above my machine to turn it off. The lamp was attached to an electric cable that could be pulled down if necessary. As I was pulling it, I got electrocuted and the shock threw me on the floor. The supervisor's box was near the electric box. He saw what happened, and in an instant, without losing control, he flicked the switch and saved my life. It turned out later that something was wrong with the insulating line. He took me aside and said to me: "You know Scheinwald, I like you, and that's why I'm telling you this. For the past few days there has been an increased number of cargo trains. They are putting Jews in locked cattle wagons and taking them to unknown destinations to execute them."

Only after the war ended did I hear about Auschwitz. We did learn from the Majdanek people that there were other extermination camps, and we heard a lot of rumors about them.

The supervisor went on to say: "There is a rumor that Polish conductors drive the locomotives to a certain spot, by the camp's gates, and then they are replaced by German conductors; the train goes into the camp and very quickly comes back empty to the same spot, where the Polish conductor takes over again. The strange thing," the supervisor continued, "is that no one hears a sound. No shooting. Nothing. I heard they burn the Jews."

Skarzysko Kamienna was a railroad intersection. We knew Jews were transported to labor camps, but what the Pole was telling me was news.

The first friend I repeated this story to was as shocked as I was. As more people heard about it, we discussed the situation among ourselves and concluded that it was impossible that the Germans were wiping out entire communities, Jewish towns and cities. We knew 6,000 or so could fill a cattle train. But we could not fathom that they were murdering children, old people, women, teenagers, men, babies, and we could not imagine that they were murdering people they could use for labor. But if not to eliminate them, why transport them to some closed camp? We did not have answers, and we did not whether to believe these stories or not. We thought it could be a piece of anti-Semitic misinformation intended to break our spirits even more. And what would we have done if we had truly believed this story? I was already a broken man in every sense, barely alive.

That was when part of the Majdanek population was transported to Skarzysko. When the first group arrived, we were shocked. They seemed to have landed from another planet. It was our first contact with human beings who had been in a death camp. They were called KL, or Konzentrationslager (concentration camp). When we heard, we each found a corner to sit and mourn, letting our tears flow. Tears fell for parents, brothers, sisters, wives, children, friends and our Jewish people.

I was helpless. I missed my family and I thought about them with great concern. At night we would sometimes sing and talk about our families. Sometimes we would cry, we knew we were living in the midst of a human tragedy. But what could we do? Each of us could die at any minute, thousands were falling; most of us could barely stand on our feet. The only thing left for us to do was to cry. How much can one cry?

We were busy searching for bread, for a piece of cloth to cover our frail bodies, and we all desperately wanted to evade the selections that were imposed on us each and every day.

The camp changed, and every day people changed, hundreds died and others were chosen to die. Some were murdered during work at the factory or inside the camp.

That was where the "hunchback" could be found. He was indeed a crooked man, well deserving of his nickname. He spoke Yiddish and spent entire days in the camp shooting people for no reason. He was a Volksdeutscher – a German born in Poland, not a Jew. One day when I was working the night shift, I heard a noise outside the barracks, and I saw a Jew trying to explain to the hunchback that he worked the night shift, which was why he was present in the camp during the day instead of being at the factory. The hunchback replied, "You're right, but I have been looking for you for a while to kill you, and now that I have found you, it's too good of an opportunity to miss." The Jew begged him not to kill him. He said his whole family had been assassinated, that he was the only one left alive, urging him to please take pity on him and let him go. This conversation took place in Yiddish. The hunchback responded, "You're really right, but you will die too, and now." Then he shot him in the face. The hunchback carried out this type of murder often and casually. He always enjoyed conversing with his victims in Yiddish prior to murdering them. He informed them he would kill them, then he did. It was a level of violence, cruelty and sadism that I cannot comprehend, coming from a sick, perverted creature who enjoyed inflicting pain and suffering on his victims and taking revenge for no reason other than his own satisfaction. We were afraid of running into him in the camp.

Many others had control over our destiny. There were kapos, who, in some camps, were Jews. The kapos controlled everything from food to labor. They could have helped us if they wanted to, although they had to be careful not to get caught. The Germans generally picked them. They wanted tall and strong figures who projected authority and who could shout. The Jewish police in the camp had served as police officers beforehand. Each barrack had a Blockältester, or barrack supervisor. In Skarzysko they were Jews, but this was not the case in every camp. These people had total control over our lives.

It is worth noting that the Germans never came into physical contact with a Jew (except when they raped Jewish girls and women). They never touched us. Movies and pictures depicting Germans helping Jews onto trains exist only in the movie makers' imagination. The police and the kapos had a holier than thou attitude and hoped to save their own skin by belittling themselves in front of the Germans. Of course, they were merely exploited by the Germans to do the dirty work.

In actuality, there was no direct contact between the Häftling – prisoner – and the kapo or police. They followed German orders first in the ghettos, then in the camps. The police tried to endear themselves to the Germans, but to the Germans we were no more than lice. They wanted us all dead. As a mere worker, I had a better chance of survival than a policeman. Our job was to produce, their job was to excel.

One winter day, when my shoes were completely worn out, and the weather was cold and harsh, friends suggested that I go to the warehouse to exchange my shoes and clothing. I knew that one day I would have no choice but to go there. I had tried to evade the issue to avoid meeting the hunchback, who was a frequent visitor at the warehouse. Now I had no choice, I was walking practically barefoot. Luckily, the monster wasn't there. I got a pair of boots with wooden soles and was so happy. I ran back to the barrack and tried them on. To my dismay, they were too tight; I could not even squeeze my foot into the boot. I had to go back to the warehouse, and to my horror, the hunchback was there. He took the boots from me, and beat me on the head with the wooden soles as hard as he could. Then he kicked me and threw me out, screaming that I should cut the boots' tip off so my toes would stick out. I took the boots and ran before he changed his mind and called me back to kill me. After I got back to the barracks, I discussed the problem with my friends. I had no choice but to take the boots apart and try to rebuild them to create some type of foot protection for myself. The alternative was to give up a ration or two of food to get shoes, but that was very dangerous. If one gave up one ration of the dirty liquid they called food, one would die. As we were talking about it, someone laughed – a rare sight in the camps – and said I would probably find a fortune, like diamonds, in those boots.

This is exactly what happened. As I was taking them apart, I found a few Zloty bills, 500 or so, and a few tens of dollars. Together, it was an incredible amount, a real fortune. That resolved my shoe situation. It was kept a secret and I managed to briefly improve my existence.

I also managed to help Sarah. She had arrived from Ozarow Kielecki. Back when I was in Ozarow on Sundays, I would bring food for Bela and Father and Sarah's family helped me. They gave me a warm house to stay in and I became friends with her brothers and met other friends through them. With time I grew to like Sarah, but the conditions for a relationship were not suitable and we both knew there would and could not be any romance under these circumstances. When I found the money in Skarzysko, I helped her as much as I could.

Later on, life separated us. During the sixties, as I was sitting in a hotel lobby in Paris, waiting for a business associate to arrive, I engaged in conversation with the hotel owner. A woman entered the lobby and immediately disappeared through a doorway. She looked familiar to me. As it turned out, the hotel owner to whom I was speaking was Sarah's husband. Sarah was alive. Our families would later meet, and a few years later she moved to Israel with her husband, where she died during a medical procedure. She left behind a son and her husband.

Later on, when I was transported to Buchenwald, I still had $10 left.

But in the meantime, we were working at night, and our situation was fraught with danger. Any German who needed manpower would come to the Jewish police and would get his men, no questions asked. Sometimes, they would coerce someone who was in the camp to go to work by flaunting their rifles. There was no return from such an experience. Many hundreds of people disappeared in such a manner from the camp, and no one ever questioned their fate.

One day, an average-sized, hermetically sealed truck entered the camp. Without reporting to the camp police, some Germans kidnapped twenty prisoners, me among them, and pushed us inside the truck. Inside it was padded with metal sheets and the door closed like a refrigerator. It could not be opened from the inside. We already knew about these trucks, which were used to execute people by having the exhaust installed in such a way that the fumes penetrated inside the truck to suffocate the passengers. They told us that if anyone tried to escape, they would eliminate us all. But luckily, this time they did not close the truck doors before they started driving. Many thoughts went through my head. Why are they taking us? Where? What do they need us for? Since the doors were open and they had not tried to gas us, maybe we would stay alive? Still, I was very scared.

After a 15-minute drive, we arrived in an area surrounded by double barbed electric wires. A building and some barracks were located between the fences, and security was tight. In our camp, the Werkschutz would watch over proceedings, but here the guards were young and tough SS men. They ordered us out of the truck. We stood and waited. In the meantime, young men appeared in the barred windows. They started singing in Polish and Yiddish. We quickly realized that they were not singing at all but chanting in Yiddish; they were informing us that they were Jewish and Polish prisoners waiting to be executed and that no one ever came out alive. Twenty minutes later, we were ordered to get back inside the truck. We were very scared when we heard these "songs", but the truck doors were again left open. Maybe this camp was connected to the death trucks, I do not know. They took us back to Skarzysko and dropped us off near the gate. I do not know why they took us on this journey. Maybe the answer has to do with a location named Bzin, mentioned in the book *Death in Yellow* by Felicia Karai. It is possible that this was what was called an Arbeitserziehungslager, or "education" labor camp.

One day, a "special situation" was declared, and we had to clean the whole camp. We overheard that someone would be visiting. As we were cleaning up, the police informed us that a Red Cross delegation would be touring the camp. It was confidential. They thought there would be some Swedes, and that was why the Germans had agreed to the visit. We were duly warned that if we were asked any questions about food, general living conditions and such, we were expected to lie and claim life was good. We were not to provide any information or clue as to real life in this camp. We were only allowed to say that we worked and were fed.

The delegation included few people; they arrived, briefly looked around the camp and left. We never heard from them again, and after their departure, things worsened. Is it believable that they remained unaffected by our appearance and hellish living conditions? Is it possible that they did not recognize the signs of genocide? Everything was clean, the food was better that one day, clothing had been distributed; it looked like after a Passover clean. Why ask questions?

The Red Cross had gone to visit other, worse camps, and did nothing about them either. Around that time, in 1944, we got another visitor, the murderer par excellence, Himmler, flanked by his troupe of SS officers. There were many rumors and much speculation surrounding this visit. In preparation for it, the Lazaret was cleaned of dirt, and of all live creatures. In Himmler's honor, we did not go to work that day. After they left, the day ended with an assembly of all the prisoners, and an extensive selection took place. At its conclusion, a few hundred Jews ended their poor existence at Werk C by the forest. The sick and weak and dying were taken care of before Himmler showed up that day. His visit was dangerous in the sense that he could have ordered the closing of the camp, wiping us out with it.

Machines were replaced in the factory, equipment was renewed, and production doubled or even tripled. Trains filled with raw materials kept arriving day and night into the camp, and we had to meet the increasing demand on the Russian front and to compensate for what the partisans destroyed. The Germans were having serious difficulties with the Russians then, and we, the slaves, had to work harder and harder. One day, military trucks arrived to take light ammunition. They did not even perform a quality control check, carried the ammunition without crates and put it directly onto the trucks. This activity continued for a few days. New transports of people were still arriving at the camp every few days. As there was an urgent need for manpower, new people were coming from other camps, including from areas near Krakow and Plaszow. In comparison with the wasted and weak human beings arriving from Majdanek, these people were "fresh" and relatively well dressed. Neither group was able to live under Skarzysko conditions nor perform the difficult labor that they were assigned.

Women had an easier time; their work was not as tough and they managed better. The "new" men fell faster than the seniors. Therefore, the camp's population never grew, on the contrary, it shrank every day. Once, a new transport had just arrived when they decided to do a selection. Just a handful of us remained alive by then. There was not enough manpower to do the job. Those we would meet in the morning at work were dead by night. Selections, starvation, sickness, a cold winter, murder... Life went on.

It was 5pm. We are standing to attention in our department, seventy men ready to go to the night shift, when Tepperman, the 35-40-year-old police chief, showed up. I was standing by a 12-liter barrel in which the "lunch" had come, and I was designated to take it back to the kitchen on our way to the factory. That day there were a number of smaller containers rather than one large barrel.

Tepperman turned to me and demanded that I open a container. Inside was a pillowcase that I had bought from a man, Moyshele, who worked in my department. I was planning to exchange the pillowcase for food with a Pole. Moyshele was a small man, and much older than me. Tepperman asked, "Where did you steal this pillowcase?" I responded, "Mr. Tepperman, you've known me for a long time, when did you ever hear talk of me stealing?" That was the truth, never throughout my existence in the camps did I steal anything, or touch anything that was not mine. He then said, "Scheinwald, don't mess with me, I want an answer by the time I have checked all the containers." He found nothing else. He became angry and ordered me out of the line. He gave me a few seconds to answer, and I repeated that I had not stolen the pillowcase. He then wanted to know who I had bought it from. That I could not tell, because I knew that if I told him, Moyshele would be executed, and possibly me too. I said I had bought it from a new person working in another department, and that I could not identify him since I did not know him well enough to recognize him. Tepperman ordered someone to bring a small bench. He said to Joseph, a policeman who was accompanying us, "Hold that dog with all your strength." Sometimes I would speak with Joseph on our march to the factory. He received more food as a policeman and also benefited from better living conditions.

Joseph placed my head between his knees, and Tepperman brought a pipe into which he inserted two electric wires. He ordered me to take my pants off and started hitting me with the pipe. He had previously beaten Joseph in the face using the same implement.

The Germans had rules, including for punishments. The standard punishment was 15 lashes, and for an especially serious "offence", 25 lashes. These were not the rules of the Jewish police. Tepperman beat me 25 times, I counted them myself. I could not take more than that, it was so painful. I did not care what the consequences would be, so pulling together all the strength left in me, I made an effort and pushed my head up, pulled Joseph away, and threw him on his back. He fell onto King Tepperman who became very angry. He started hitting Joseph and called out to another two policemen. They held me down, and Tepperman continued with the beatings. I could not count anymore; my friends did it for me. After giving me 52 lashes, he got tired and left with my pillowcase. My friends helped me up and dragged me to work. My back was covered in wounds. Pinhas Feinshtat was one of those who helped me. He was a religious man, and we remained good friends until the end of the war.

They were now doing selections simultaneously at the factory and camp. First, they asked nicely who felt weak or ill, and told them to step forward. We were told the sick would be transferred to a recovery camp before there was serious shortage of labor; they needed to strengthen the weak to then send them back to work. A father – Benjamin – and his two sons were in the department at that time. Benjamin was from Stopnica, and he encouraged one of his sons to step forward because he was not feeling well. When I saw that a father was pushing his son forward, without thinking I stepped forward too. After all, a father is older, wiser, so surely, he knew better. I felt two hands pulling me backwards. In the meantime, Benjamin's son and someone else were led away to stand with the rest of the weak and sick.

Krzepicki was marching towards us. He especially loved to murder women. He said he had seen someone else step forward and wanted to know who it was. We denied all knowledge of any such thing. Tepperman was not there, and the woman murderer left us alone. I managed to survive another selection. It was Pinhas, who later on lived in Toronto, who was my savior that day.

As these selections were going on, the police were searching the barracks. Those found there, along with the sick who were brought from the infirmary, those who had stepped forward and hundreds of other Jews were led away by the armed guards of the Werkschutz to Werk C where they were exterminated, as usual.

Some tend to blame the police in its entirety, but one has to discriminate. Not everyone behaved like the police in Skarzysko. As I understand it, those young people, most of whom came from nice, good homes, would have normally gone to university, become professionals, traders etc. if not for the war, but the situation led them to do things they would have never done under different circumstances. They were pushed into it and could not get out without jeopardizing their lives. By doing their duty, they thought they would be protected from the Nazis.

When the Germans started demanding more of them than to just keep the order – which was the primary job of the police – it was too late, and they had to carry out their humiliating tasks. There were many who deserted or fled, or even cooperated with the underground. Yet, most went on doing their job because perhaps even in hell it was easier to be a policeman instead of a Jew being led to his death. Over time, they also paid with their lives.

Some of them mistreated us as they lost control over themselves and considered us animals. They thought they could steal from us and get away with it, which they did. Sometimes they murdered people for money, or they would threaten to denounce someone arbitrarily in order to steal from them. Their day also arrived, and they too were exterminated. They too were murdered by their masters, the Germans. I am certain most of them were not born criminals. The great majority of them were probably decent people who got entangled in this tragedy and could not escape the web. Still, they came out as murderers and traitors.

In camps like Treblinka, there was no Jewish police but there were kapos. Their job was very similar to the job of the police in the ghetto. The difference was that Treblinka was a designated extermination camp, whereas the labor camps – though acting as death camps – were supposedly intended for labor. Some of the kapos behaved well. They organized the Treblinka uprising which caused the destruction and closing of the whole camp. They took the risk knowing in advance that they would face death if they were found. They managed nonetheless to take revenge and even kill some Germans. Part of the camp was burned, hundreds managed to flee – it was an uprising worth the name.

Our life was not becoming easier. It was never enough for the Germans to conduct a "small" selection of 100 to 200 people. Hundreds and hundreds of people had to be chosen and often, in just a couple of hours, thousands of lives evaporated. There was not one week without selections. Not one. Sometimes we had two selections in one week.

Statistics do not account for those who tried to flee, those who died different types of deaths, those from outside the camp who were eliminated in the camp. I do not speak of suicides, because there were very few. As the pressure mounted, as conditions worsened, those who had managed to survive decided to keep going until the end, if only to see the fall of the German monster.

Ignoring political excuses, until today, I do not understand why it took so long for the world we had counted on to overcome Germany. It is clear that no one minded the murder of Jews too much, and that, really, no one lost sleep over the elimination of my people. No one was in a hurry to save us from the atrocities. This is why the war continued for nearly six years and that is why six million Jewish people were slaughtered.

We could, for example, have expected the Russians to do more than stop their armies in the middle of Poland, waiting until the last Jew had perished. But they had signed a treaty with Nazi Germany, the Ribbentrop-Molotov agreement. Similar and worse approaches were taken by Western countries. Everyone had plenty of time to think while we were being murdered. I am not attempting to solve my personal problems with the Western world, but I cannot tell my story if I ignore what went through our heads during the war. We were completely helpless. Those who had power, strength and means sat in silence and watched the Germans fulfill their dreams. It was not just Nazis killing Jews, it was the German people in its entirety. Everyone cooperated to achieve a successful outcome to their Jewish problem. They were 80 million, it was impossible to hide these facts and we paid the price.

Despite fighting a war on several fronts, they were also waging war against helpless, battered Jews – against babies, toddlers, children, their parents and their grandparents. They did not give up on extinguishing even one life, even a baby's life, they refused to spare the soul of even one human being. Their war was a war against the Jews. All Jews.

And then, there was the Jewish police and creatures like Krzepicky, who continued to show up when we stood to attention every morning and kidnapped women who arrived late for work. He would catch a woman at random, throw her between the barbed wires, wait until thousands of innocent inmates had passed through the gate. Then he would pull up her skirt or dress, and if she wore underwear, he would take it off and then he would start beating her, at least 15 lashes. Each and every day, he would find victims, sometimes more than one, and he always went through this same procedure. The women would start bleeding, cry and scream from pain, and he would order them to go back to their department accompanied by a policeman and additional beatings. Sometimes he would kill them, depending on his mood. After this daily routine, he would have his breakfast, and even when we moved to the large camp marked by two signs, in Polish and German, "Judenarbeitslager" – Jewish Labor Camp – he would continue with his sick and murderous activities.

Many others acted similarly. They were faithful servants to their German masters, and each served in a different capacity. Milsztein, for example, was the informer. He would provide the Germans with any information they wanted and tell on everyone. Sometimes he blackmailed people and demanded money, gold, anything he could get his hands on, anything they could or couldn't give him, and after he had blackmailed them, he went to the Germans anyway. They in turn executed the persons involved. Now, what is really the use of people you can no longer blackmail? What is the use of someone who has nothing left to give? The new transports would bring Jews who sometimes still had some possessions, so they would steal from them before killing them.

There was another boss, Albirt, who commanded the civilian camp. In fact, he had no job. Since the camp was under Gestapo control, his position was not clear and until today I do not know exactly what he was doing there. I think he provided the Germans with women, but I have no proof. He was a quiet man in his forties, and well dressed. My friend Leon claims he also held some job at the Schlieben camp. Supposedly, he was the Jewish camp representative. He did not get involved in police affairs. He would wander around and never touched any prisoners, but there was always the feeling he was up to something bad. He had a good relationship with the Germans; they would go out together at night and have fun with women that the Germans would execute at the end of the night's entertainment. They did not want anyone to inform the Gestapo about what was going on so they left no witnesses. Albirt did talk to us on occasion and was more flexible in his attitude. He was not afraid of the Nazis, or so it seemed. We had no hard evidence that Albirt directly hurt us, but it seems certain that through his associations and connections many Jews died. Due to lack of evidence, he was not convicted in the Buchenwald trials, which I will discuss later.

Other people who caused much pain and harm and death were those who stole from others. One must realize that a piece of clothing, a couple of dollars, a few Zlotys counted as a fortune in the camp. With that, someone could save their life but it could also be their death sentence. Some people lost their moral compass and stole from other inmates.

Bertenschlager was the Gestapo commander of the camp and feared by all. He was a tall and slim Nazi with slouching shoulders. He wore the black Gestapo uniform and a hat with a skull on it; his boots shone, and he always carried a gun and a whip. He loved to crack the whip in the air and listen to the sound. More than that, he loved to use the whip on people. He did not "visit" us often, but when he entered the camp, we knew he was up to something. We knew we would pay dearly. He was not hesitant with his gun either. If the gun jammed, there was always a volunteer who jumped at the occasion and offered his own gun. After he left, it was like watching the dark skies and waiting for a storm. We feared new instructions, changes, tortures he had concocted. He was seriously professional in his murderous ways. Despite the fact that we were in a HASAG-owned camp, the regime managed to instill terror and spread death among us with the help of sub-animals like Bertenschlager.

Moshe Finger and Lola counted among the thieves, and I am sure Gnat was not exactly a saint either. Everyone stole from us, everyone beat us up, everyone was a strong, courageous hero against the weak, the starved, the tired, the lonely. Even those who wanted to help could not save many lives, but there were those whose sheer behavior caused the murder of thousands of others.

We were wiped out for no good reason, it was completely aimless. They tortured us just for the sake of it; no one even paid attention anymore. The worst part is that the Germans rarely set foot in this camp. They were not interested in what was going on there, so what was the point of torture? Even the perpetrators could not save themselves in the end. Only a handful of Jewish culprits managed to stay alive; after the war, they were targeted by survivors. I witnessed a lynching in Austria after someone screamed in the street that he had seen a kapo. In Rome, where I was with Simcha Janowski, a friend I met during the war, we looked for a synagogue. We met a group of people who sent us to the Joint, which in turn sent us to Cine Città. During a conversation with this group, one of them pointed to someone and said, "You were a kapo." They started beating him up. It turned out he had not been a kapo – there were a few cases of mistaken identity.

I have been trying to figure out why they acted in this manner, to get into the heads of these monstrous creatures, many of whom were Jews after all, at a time when the Germans attempted to wipe the Jewish people off the face of the earth. It was known that when the Germans eliminated the ghettos, they also eliminated their servants, conspirators and collaborators. These people knew their chance of survival was close to zero. The Germans left no trace, not one survivor, everyone knew that. They did too. So what was the point?

During the Buchenwald trials, Milsztein in his defense said to the judges that he had been a kid, he had not understood what he was doing, he was merely following orders. But Dr. Sacks, a mature man in his thirties, he was no longer a child, and all the rest, why did they torture and kill us? Why? It was not enough that the Germans, Poles, Ukrainians, Lithuanians and all the rest were slaughtering us, the Jews had a go too; they closed the circle.

A famous person who knew what was expected of him was Czerniakow. He was the head of the Jewish community, the Judenrat, in the Warsaw ghetto. He understood he had no chance, no matter what road he took, and committed suicide with his family. I never supported this act. I think he was a traitor. It was a question of personal honor, but not an honorable gesture towards his people. There was no leadership and no dignity. He should have gone to the young people in Warsaw, told them the truth and tried to organize a resistance. Then, perhaps, we could have done something. But he chose to make his life easier by committing suicide. It is a pity that he chose this path, because perhaps he could have organized a rebellion when there was still time.

However, it is clear that no one person or group could have changed the fate of the Jewish people under German occupation. We are all so smart in retrospect and come up with "easy" solutions regarding what should have been done. Then, everything was hard and complicated. But the fact of the matter is that even a little help then could have achieved a lot, souls could have been saved. Like me, Pinhas Feinshtat survived, Szachne Gerstein survived and Leon Goldblum too; we were all Skarzysko "graduates". I have no doubt in my mind that one of the main reasons why we survived is because we helped each other, we were responsible for one another and willing to do anything for each other.

At some point in 1944 we started hearing encouraging rumors from the outside about the situation at the front, but conditions in the camp were horrendous. We often thought the solution was to escape, but I was against it. When the Germans started eliminating the ghettos and sending Jews to death camps, I understood that the only way to survive, if at all possible, was to adjust. If I was not going to be able to survive in the camp, I would not make it anywhere, or so I thought.

Something that I did not know at the time was that my older brother Hersh (Zvi in Hebrew), who had so much in common with the Poles, and whose chance of survival we thought was high, had been murdered after he had realized he had no choice but to flee from his hiding place near Ozarow. He was killed along with a group of his friends, all from Sochaczew, in spring 1943 in a village called Beilin. Sometimes I regretted not having him with me in the hell called Skarzysko, maybe he would have survived there after all.

Successful escapes were rare. I remember that one day in Skarzysko, we were delayed in going to work because two young men had tried to escape. They were soon caught in the train station. They were brought back, and with their hands tied behind their back, they were forced to kneel. Bertenschlager did the honors. He took out his gun and shot one of them. When he pulled the trigger to shoot the other, the gun did not work. He tried again but it would not shoot, so he had to take a gun from a friend of his to kill the second man.

The executioners had no rules to follow. You had to kill, that was the most important task, a big accomplishment, the highest purpose. The rest was irrelevant. That is why, in my opinion, we had no chance of surviving if we fled and were caught. It is true that some people managed to escape successfully, and even Germans helped them sometimes, not knowing they were Jews. Generally, Germans could not differentiate between us and the Poles. Part of the tragedy is that two million Poles were massacred. How cynical, especially in view of what the Poles did to us. It was well worth it for them to sacrifice two million or even more of their own as long as the Jews were eliminated. The goal was to have a Poland free of Jews at all costs. Obviously, there was no punishment for the murder of Jews, by Poles or others, and many gladly helped. The Armja Krajowa did it in an organized manner.

All of this contributed to why I felt I had to find means of survival within the camp. It is not the only reason I survived. I really have no answer as to why I remained alive. I do not know how or why, but it is not because I am smarter, and it is not because I am different from anyone else. It is not because I was a hero. We were not heroes. We were young and we wanted to live.

People were killed to make room for new transports. New people were robbed of whatever they had and then murdered. We heard that the Russian army was getting closer. That was good. But we also heard that if they advanced too fast, they would destroy the camp and us with it. Under these circumstances, the underground managed to infiltrate the factory. The AK recruited Polish and Jewish workers to get ammunition out. Some Jews contributed to and helped the Polish underground, despite everything.

One day, we stood to attention in the assembly area – Appellplatz – which was heavily guarded by armed Werkschutz soldiers. Poles were being erected. They brought over a young Jewish man and read a "verdict", a sentence decreed by the military court in Radom, where it had been decided to hang this man. They asked for a volunteer to hang him, and when no one offered, they ordered one of us to come out of the ranks. The person chosen for this job started crying, and continued sobbing as he placed the rope around his friend's neck.

It was then that in a matter of about 20 minutes, his hair turned completely gray right before our eyes. We were then informed that this would be the fate of all Polish underground collaborators, and of anyone caught stealing or committing acts of sabotage.

There was no precedent to reading a verdict. Of course, they never brought a Jew before a German court. The Germans may have needed some type of testimony against Poles, which increased the hatred the Poles felt towards the Jews, who supposedly testified against the underground movement. Evidently, the Poles had conveniently chosen to forget that the Jew in Appellplatz had worked for the Polish underground and paid with his life. In Radom, the Poles supposedly saw him testify in a German courtroom. It was all a show in order to sentence hundreds of people to death. While we were standing to attention in the camp, twenty people from the plant were taken by the Germans and hung by their necks in trees. The Germans put signs on them indicating the same fate would happen to saboteurs and thieves. They remained hanging there for a number of hours, and after they were taken down work continued as usual.

The Russian army continued to advance and we started hearing from Germans and others that repairs were needed at the front and that the Germans had retreated in some areas. It was then that they started playing marching music over the loudspeakers across the camp. We began to feel a change in the atmosphere. Not that they stopped the killings, of course, or the selections, or that transports were not arriving, but we sensed it was the beginning of the end of this camp; we could feel it in the air.

1944 began full of hope with many victories on the Russian front, and we often heard encouraging words from the Poles who said the war was nearing its end, that the Russians were coming, but these words were a small consolation for us. We continued to starve, to be sick, to be beaten and to be butchered. The pressure put on us to increase productivity was unbearable. The Germans needed more and more ammunition their servants performed their tasks faithfully. Some did their duty for their homeland, the Reich, the Führer, for a land free of Jews. We were everyone's scapegoat. During one of our shifts, as we were coming to work, I noticed there were no Poles. We felt, without understanding exactly why, that something was changing. Then we heard that the Russians were quickly advancing near the Vistula, a river that traverses Poland from north to south. It runs close to Skarzysko. We were afraid the camp would be destroyed, that we would be put in the tunnel and blown up. But we continued our forced labor as if nothing was happening. One day, as we were getting ready to march to the plant, they ordered us to get into formation. Something caused a delay and we were not moving. They started a selection, but different from those we were familiar with. They selected whole departments, mine among them; we realized it was not a murder selection but something else. We were ordered to march to the railroad tracks. People from the police were with us, as was Mr. Finger and his wife Lola and Albirt himself. We understood we were going on a transport to an unknown destination. It was clear that after twenty-seven months of barely existing in this hell called Skarzysko Kamienna, Werk A, I was leaving it. In my estimation, over 100,000 Jews had been murdered in Skarzysko Kamienna in those twenty-seven months. They are various estimates to the number of Jews killed there. I was there from beginning to end, and I can testify that no less than 100,000 were murdered in Skarzysko.

Sadly, I still did not know where I was going and was very scared of the unknown. We knew what had happened to previous transports of Jews but had no choice. We did not know what to expect from the new place they were taking us to, or if we would even make it there alive. Hope helped us fight against starvation, suffering, cold, heat and pain. The thought that the Russians would soon win the war kept us alive. It was all fantasy, the product of German misinformation. One needed courage to continue surviving and not give up. One could not live on hope alone, but those who lost hope could not survive.

We were ordered to dismantle the barracks and put the parts on the train. We knew we would be transported on the same train as we got organized to leave towards what we thought would be another camp. The Jewish police was packing their clothing and gathering their food. We sensed they knew where we were heading. It was always possible that the Germans had lied to them about our destination, but what choice did we have? We could not change a thing. We were ordered onto the train. We had previously put straw in the cattle wagon taken from the planks on which we had slept. It was filthy and crawling with bugs and lice. We mounted the train in our work groups. The Werkschutz checked to make sure there were at least eighty people in each cattle wagon. The numbers did not match what the Germans had, and so they added different "service" people to the wagons to make sure no wagon contained fewer than eighty persons. The Jewish police climbed aboard a separate wagon which had already been prepared for them with fresh straw and some supplies. There was an opening of about 30 to 40 centimeters in length in each upper corner of the wagon. On the way to the unknown, the Jewish police continued to act as before; they gave orders, they controlled food distribution, they closed the wagons. The Werkschutz guarded the train, the same ones who had guarded the plant.

A large group of prisoners remained in the camp, the rumor being that they were meant to dismantle the whole plant. Part of the Jewish infrastructure also remained. Later on, the Germans learned that they had made a mistake. For political reasons, the Russians had stopped advancing. They started reorganizing the plant to resume production, but most of those who could do the work were already gone, as was part of the equipment.

In August/September 1944, they closed the camp for good and sent everyone to another HASAG plant, Czestochowa in Poland. From there, many later arrived in Germany.

When Skarzysko closed and the machines were turned off, a few Jewish men hid in those that had been used to heat up steel, hoping to escape after the last transport had left the camp. Tragically, as the Russians were approaching, the Poles decided to turn the machines back on, burning the Jews alive.

Before the doors closed we had received our bread ration and some other food. That was a good sign, but you never knew. The train started moving and we were on our way to somewhere. The general direction was western. It took two days to cross the German border and we understood that we were not headed for a death camp in Poland. There was still a lot of fear, we knew that the presence of Jewish police within our ranks on the wagon was of no significance whatsoever. We were filled with doubt and questions. If I remember correctly, this transport consisted of men only. They were still not transporting women from Skarzysko.

I am thinking of the twenty-seven months of captivity in Skarzysko, this hell on earth. What was Skarzysko for me? A camp which stole twenty-seven months out of my young life and stole the precious lives of innumerable human beings. Those who survived were maimed forever, and in many ways remained invalids. Although on the surface they may work, have new families, function in some way or fashion, they are dead people who happen to walk on their two feet. To my knowledge, according to my understanding, this was one of the worst camps that existed, death camps included. Perhaps it was the worst among them. Skarzysko was the most horrible camp. In relative numbers, as many Jews were murdered there as in other death camps. To the extent that German and Polish archives and documentation exist, no figure reflects accurately the real number of human beings annihilated in Skarzysko. Their interest is in historical revisionism, to minimize the true reporting on the number of prisoners that were held there and the number of murders. I have read that they even shortened the actual time Skarzysko existed. These sources are not trustworthy.

The real count must be derived from those who witnessed camp existence personally, physically, who were there and survived. We must share the suffering we endured at the hands of those who had power over us. We have to recount the suffering by those who are no longer here to tell their own stories. More than once I wanted to die, but I also wanted revenge on those who killed my family, my people, my soul. I am not saying that every day of my current life is happy, but I managed to raise a family, and I succeeded in doing what my mother asked me to do. I stayed alive to remind the world about what they did to us and what they are still trying to do. I am a walking memorial to those who were assassinated. This is my revenge. The revenge of my brothers and sisters, my mother and father, my whole family who is not here anymore.

Skarzysko should be treated like any other camp despite the fact that it was independently run, corporate-owned, and had Jewish police. It was not a Jewish ghetto with a Rabbi and his followers. We had no rest, no food, no dignity. We did not get to share Jewish holidays, there were no intrigues or political struggles that allowed us to reach powerful positions and change our own governing bodies. It was not business as usual as some may claim. Those who say Skarzysko was a straightforward labor camp are fantasizing and do not understand the reality or dimensions of the place. Our living conditions, from food rationing to the work and everything in between, only worsened over time. Nobody ever helped us. Not the Red Cross. Not anyone. It must be understood that this was a large ammunition manufacturing plant where Jewish slaves were toiling away, not one of them of their own free will. Jews lived and suffered in this camp, and had to fight for their existence, for a piece of bread, for a rag with which to cover themselves, for some clothing for their frail and emaciated bodies; all this without breaking down. And without falling victim to the constant death selections.

We all had a small metal tin hanging from our belts. The belt consisted only of a piece of wire, but you had to be ready to receive food at any time. The food ration was always small and the piece of bread never more than 200 grams, most often 150 grams (the equivalent of 5-7 oz). We were given only enough food to keep us breathing. Karai claims that we had work tickets, which I do not recall. Where would we have put them? Our existence was split between the factory department where we worked and the barracks where we slept.

We spoke a lot about some help that would never come, but we were foolishly hopeful especially around the Red Cross visit. Nothing came of that. If any attempt to help took place, it was stopped at the top somewhere and never reached us. In Werk C, where executions took place, many would be assassinated, including people from the outside like some Poles. But the Poles worked hard in getting rid of the Jews, at the price of their own blood. It is on Polish land that many death camps were created, nowhere else.

As we got information from the underground about places like Plaszow, Majdanek and Oswiecim, our suspicions were reinforced. Some people tried to flee, but we thought that our chances of survival would increase if we stayed in the camp itself. I am not aware of massive escapes from camps, only individual ones. Most were caught and executed. Many by the Poles themselves.

We lost control over our lives and destinies. Not one step could be taken of our free will. We could not decide to sleep, to get up, to wash, to use the toilets, nothing. We did not make one move without being ordered to do so. We simply were not allowed. It creates a sense of humiliation, degradation and helplessness when a grown-up person cannot urinate or defecate without receiving an order to stand in line for the toilets. It was depressing that some low-life criminal controlled our every move and every breath.

This was the end of my sad Skarzysko Kamienna epoch.

HASAG is not generally known to the public. It was a small company and many Germans were not and are still not familiar with it. It stood in the shadow of large manufacturing firms that produced weapons and ammunitions such as Krupp and Roechling, which people remembered from the First World War. When Hitler came to power and started manufacturing weapons at an unprecedented pace Krupp and Roechling were in the picture, as was HASAG. In 1939, the latter employed 4,000 people, but still counted as a relatively small war-time company. Its break came when Germany invaded Poland, and factories were set up in Skarzysko and Czestochowa.

HASAG then signed a contract with the German government and received the manufacturing plants in Kielce, becoming the

Wehrmacht's largest and leading provider of ammunition for the Russian front. Towards the end of the war they "employed" over 150,000 people in Leipzig alone. It was a huge company, even by German standards. After the Germans retreated from Poland in 1944, HASAG's plants continued to operate in Leipzig, Schlieben, Flossberg, Herzberg and so forth. Manufacturing continued until the very end of the war when director Paul Budin committed suicide by explosion in the Leipzig plant. With the demise of the German dream to rule the world for the next 1,000 years came the demise of HASAG.

Paul Budin was a member of the Nazi party. He was loyal to the party and to Hitler and through his connections, HASAG made a name for itself among the major manufacturing plants. Budin's personal connections led to government commissions, and HASAG also managed to get land in Poland relatively close to Russia, which shortened transportation routes and lowered expenses. All the regime needed was for the manufacturing and distribution of ammunition and weapons to proceed at full speed. The items HASAG produced included 75mm, 100mm and 150mm explosives, bullets, explosives and personal anti-tank weapons. There were other manufacturers that were much larger that received mutually profitable contracts after the conquest of Poland. They included Reichswerke Hermann Goering and I.G. Farbenindustrie. These plants operated on the back of Jewish manpower, which represented the largest chunk of the workforce in the weapons plants.

Although these firms needed strong and healthy people to do slave labor for them, they did not provide the workers with even minimum working conditions. They exploited them until the end. These workers received no food to eat, no clothes to wear, they worked in closed camps, were separated from family members, worked 12-hour shifts day and night, all on 800 calories per day. They worked seven days a week, never had a day off, never had a rest; in some of these camps people worked in underground tunnels and did not see the light of day for months on end. They never received medical treatment, not even basic first aid. There was no medication at all.

The mortality rate was sky high, and if we add to that the effort put in by the Ukrainians to kill workers, people fell like flies. How did this fit in with HASAG's financial interests? After a short while, the manpower they had been given was trained and knew its job. Wouldn't it be in the firm's best interest to keep their slaves healthy and more productive? To lower turnover by providing better conditions? I estimate that the lifespan of a worker in Skarzysko and Schlieben was a week to a couple of weeks. It was not even a few days in Flossberg. Schlieben was a camp worse than Skarzysko, and Flossberg worse than Schlieben and the transports worse than both.

This is how, in collaboration with HASAG, the Nazi regime turned a "labor" camp into a death camp. These camps were extermination camps without gas chambers and crematoria. It seems that the killing of Jews was more pressing than the manufacturing of arms and ammunition for their holy war and far more important than any economic interests. That was the moral standard of the Germans who participated in this death orgy.

Paul Budin, who I am certain was a smart and talented businessman, used his SS connections and invited Himmler and some of the highest-ranking officials of this regime to visit the small and unknown Skarzysko camp. Even Budin did not think it was necessary to change anything, even if only to increase productivity and better financial bottom lines. The idea was not to give civilians work, occupying them in a constructive manner and saving their lives in the process, even if there was an element of exploitation. It is clear that there were no conflicts in their minds between the financial well-being of the company and the elimination of their manpower. Hundreds of thousands of human beings. It was sacrosanct to get rid of the Jews. The rest was perhaps important, but secondary. The idea was to get rid of an unwanted population whose talent and energy they first tapped to death. Therefore, HASAG, Reichswerke Hermann Goering, I.G. Farbenindustrie, Deutsche Bank and hundreds of other large and small German companies cooperated fully with this murderous regime.

Can this be understood using logic? Can a normal person understand it?

The scope of the systematic killing by Ukrainians and others was immense. The camp was a well-oiled death machine. While we were exploited until our last breath for their own war needs, they killed us and kept killing us. The number of survivors from HASAG camps is miserably small. There is no one left to tell the world about this tragedy. Those in the camps were coerced to endure countless types of torture and humiliation unknown to mankind before 1933.

Leaving Skarzysko, we were on a train that moved very slowly. That was fine by us, we had all the time in the world, no place to go and no one to rush to. Maybe a miracle would happen and the Russians would get there first and liberate us. Maybe. But dreams are not stronger than suffering.

The train was slow, the wagon was locked, and the view that someone perhaps managed to see from the small corner air vent was dull. Our worries centered on our future and what torture still awaited us. Since we had so much time and did not need to stand to attention, I kind of dozed off and allowed myself to think about my father. Where was he? Where were all my brothers and sisters? Would I ever see them again? I became every sad, and saw no point in living. Behind me was complete destruction, and I was so alone in the world. I did not have one soul close to me anywhere in the world, my youth was ruined and my education had been cut short. I was now being schooled in the camps; all that I had seen so far were murder and endless crimes. With such an education, how could I cope and keep on living if I ever made it out of this hell?

My head was filled with these thoughts and as I dozed, I tried to find something in my mind that I could grasp. There was plenty of time. I thought of what would be, and how, if, and when this nightmare would be over. There was not enough food; food did not exist in my poor, miserable world. I was sad, and bored, and I felt uncomfortable. The lice were eating me alive, the bugs were not letting go. Then the train stopped and we heard German being spoken, not Polish like before. We had crossed the border into Germany. We also heard sirens, and occasionally war planes and bombs being dropped. We started thinking that perhaps, after all, the end was near. Wherever they opened the train's heavy doors, life did not seem so pastoral. We saw small, well-kept houses in far-away villages, and on occasion, someone running away from houses destroyed by bombs. Here we only felt war, and it showed itself too.

The train pulled into a small station called Weimar. It stopped for a few minutes and then continued. We felt that something had happened. We stopped again and the doors were opened. Everyone got out and the group started gathering around fields and lightly wooded areas. It looked like a nice place. We were ordered to walk along the railroad tracks and in a few minutes we discovered a gate to a camp. We were familiar with all of this, and we were scared. The transport had lasted a day and we were now in front of a camp we had heard about before the war: Buchenwald. When I arrived at Buchenwald, I still had the $10 that I had found in the boots at Skarzysko Kamienna. Upon arrival, I shred the bill into small pieces, into crumbs, waiting for a decision to be made about our lives.

The entrance gates to Buchenwald were decorated with the famous wrought iron sign: "Jedem das Seine", meaning to each his own, or everyone gets what they deserve. It was scary to walk through these gates but there was nothing we could do about it. In a matter of minutes, we were standing at the entrance to the gas chambers. We had heard about them from other inmates and we were starting to wonder if all the pain, suffering, torture and dehumanization had been endured merely for us to end our young lives here, at this critical stage of the war, so near the end. Here the fence around the camp was electric, the guards were SS and it was the end of the road. I sank into my thoughts and suddenly heard an order to sit down. To my great surprise, it was civilian Jews who had given the order and we could see no soldier or policeman except for in the guard towers.

Some people who did not look too bad physically, who did not seem to weigh 35 kilos (77 pounds) like we did, turned to us. They addressed us politely in Yiddish and said they knew where we were coming from and promised that here nothing would happen to us. They told us we would be sent to a labor camp outside the camp and that we should not be afraid. But we had heard the same thing before and received many such promises. They were meant to calm us down but most of the time they were pure lies.

We were sitting in the Appellplatz asked who among us had authority roles in Skarzysko, who managed the camp, who was a high-ranking staff member. Of course, we were afraid to tell them, because we did not yet know whether they would be able to hurt us again. When the civilians saw that we remained silent and were not willing to divulge the police personnel among us, they tried to identify them themselves.

They walked across the tiles right in front of the gas chambers and then suddenly someone got up and put the police hat on his head. Spontaneously, everyone started identifying the police staff including Tepperman, Krzepicki, Albirt, with their nice clothing and their packages of food. The latter were quickly opened and all the food found inside divided up among us. The policemen were made to take their boots and clothes off and stood there naked like the day they were born. Then they were led towards the gas chambers to be shaved, washed and disinfected with Carbol, a Lysol-like product. After they left, we got organized and they started giving us bread, a large portion, with jam or a piece of sausage. We each received some soap and a towel. That immediately decreased our confidence because we knew the soap and towel could only mean they wanted us to be calm and do what we were told without resisting or creating panic. That way they could send us to the gas chambers quietly and efficiently, and from there to the crematorium; this whole charade had been planned just to deceive us.

Could we have done anything about it? It bothers me that we were so helpless. We were weak, exhausted and hungry, we had no energy or strength or desire to live. We dragged ourselves towards the gas chambers while the civilians kept repeating that they would not harm us, and that everything would be fine. To show their good faith, they accompanied us to the gas chambers.

Later, I learned that these civilians had themselves been candidates for the crematorium.

We entered a huge room where barbers were standing around. They shaved our whole bodies until not one hair was left and then we were smeared with a disinfectant that burned our skin. They smeared it everywhere, in every crevice, every intimate part of our frail bodies, with commercial paint brushes. Following this painful treatment, we indeed felt better, and we knew we were free of parasites and bugs and other animals. Our clothing was burned with the straw from the wagons.

This is how we were separated from what little we had and a new miserable chapter of our lives began. We had no idea how this chapter would end.

We walked into the gas chambers in groups. I was standing there knowing that no one ever came out alive. There were two sets of doors, one to enter, one to take the corpses out to the crematorium. The doors were left open, and we heard some rustling noise. Everyone expected gas to come out of the pipes. Instead a strong stream of water, hard to believe but it was true, real water, no gas, flowed. Warm water! And we had soap! We washed ourselves happily and for a brief moment, we forgot our hunger and our fears. We scrubbed ourselves with the soap, stood under the warm water, and then we were told that on the count of ten they would turn off the showers. We rinsed off the lather and proceeded to the adjacent room. There, every orifice of our bodies was checked for gold, money and valuables as SS men watched from the sidelines to make sure we were free of disease. I was happy that they did not find anything on me. We were handed striped uniforms and a number. It was the first time I had received a number as a prisoner. I was now officially an inmate of a concentration camp, not just a labor camp prisoner. I no longer knew where my friends were, including Leon.

We were then taken to the camp. Near the area of the political prisoners there was an empty long barrack, and we were informed it was designated for us. They explained the sleeping arrangements to ensure the barrack would contain 1,800 people. The curfew was 10pm, when we would be ordered to lay on the hard ground pressed against each other with everyone facing in the same direction, like sardines. At night, they would wake us up and order us to turn to the other side, all 1,800 human beings simultaneously.

We received a bowl of soup and were ordered to stand to attention as the SS men counted us to make sure our number matched the number on their documentation. Then they ordered us to go to sleep, the wake-up call would be at 5.30am. We would have to stand in formation, and we were told some of us would be sent to work. Those who could testify against the previous police staff at Skarzysko were to remain behind and report to the camp office.

Those who had had any type of management role in Skarzysko were held under arrest and investigated by Jewish judges. A team of Buchenwald prisoners had organized trials against Skarzysko personnel accused of mistreating us, taking place in the barrack where we slept. We were told the trials would be conducted by inmates who had been actual judges, that the defendants would receive inmates – ex-lawyers – to represent them and that the court would decide the verdict and sentence after hearing all sides. We were told that we had to testify, and that we should not be afraid because the defendants would not harm us again.

We were surprised when they asked us about the police, and they told us they knew what had gone on in Skarzysko. In Buchenwald, many of the prisoners were part of the intelligentsia – including Leon Blum – and there were lawyers and judges among them. We were shocked to hear the police from Skarzysko was going to be indicted and tried. Thirteen people were convicted and sentenced to death. I think they later convicted additional police members from Skarzysko, as more arrived with new transports. The Buchenwald prisoners tried the Skarzysko police because they were Jewish. They took it upon themselves to provide some level of justice within our own people. The Germans did not get involved and did not care.

Only a few people registered to testify. Most were hesitant. Three of four days after our arrival, we were informed during the morning formation that the trials would commence. All witnesses were to stay and not go to work. Three judges presided at a table. The first defendant was Tepperman, whom many people testified against, including me. The judge asked him why he had given me 52 sadistic lashes, and Tepperman answered that I had stolen something.

"First, I do not believe Scheinwald stole anything. You had no evidence whatsoever of his guilt. Besides, what right do you have to punish anyone?" replied the judge.

"I was the head of the police, and it was my job."

"Didn't you know you could have killed him with these beatings?"

"I knew, but I had to do my job."

"So why so many lashes? 52 lashes? If a German would have punished him, it would have been 15 lashes."

"Because Scheinwald beat me and caused me to fall," answered Tepperman.

Then they called Joseph who had forcibly held me down. He testified to what happened, backing up my account and reminding Tepperman that he had beaten him too on some occasion. After some ten other witnesses had taken the stand, the court informed us that the verdict would be read shortly.

There was no evidence against Albirt. Although all the Skarzysko prisoners knew he was the king of crime, there were no testimonies or evidence against him. He was "freed" to become a prisoner like the rest of us in this concentration camp.

A couple of days later we were called to the barrack for the reading of the verdicts. Six were found guilty and sentenced to death, among them Tepperman, who was immediately lynched. He was beaten to death. Having no stones or sticks to kill him with, we used wooden shoe soles to beat him to death. Krzepicky was ordered to commit suicide on the electric fence, and the "boy" Milsztein was also sentenced to die. In the general excitement, he was pushed into the toilet hole where he expired. All the rest were sent to be guinea pigs for medical experiments in the camp, and it can safely be assumed that none of them came out alive.

I am not sorry about their death. They had hundreds of people that they had killed directly or indirectly on their conscience, if they had one. They had collaborated with the Germans and taken deadly initiative too often, performing acts of violence that were not required of them. They sent people to violent deaths to satisfy their own cruel desires and caused sadistic suffering without justification. Therefore, their punishment was well deserved and represented but a modicum of the justice we were entitled to. Unfortunately, many people did not live to be liberated, but at least this was a drop of revenge.

From following transports that arrived from Skarzysko and Czestochowa (a town sacred to the Poles: HASAG was located there and also had a local subsidiary), seven others were tried and given the death penalty, including the infamous Dr. Sacks, Finger and Lola.

Most of Skarzysko's "graduates" and their masters had now been spread around various labor camps. Some had fled before boarding the train to Germany and the great majority was murdered under different circumstances. Very few survived Skarzysko Kamienna; just a handful of people remained alive.

All day the Germans would read numbers on the loudspeakers. The numbers corresponded to human beings who had to report to their death in the gas chambers. The Germans would also put marching music on, or some propaganda. They did not enter the camp itself. They sat in offices outside; only one of them entered, stick in hand, during assembly.

In Buchenwald, they did not use us as manpower. They only took groups of prisoners for work, about 500 out of 2,000. Some people were also sent to be used for medical experiments. The only thing that interested the Germans was the body count during assembly and the number of dead.

Those who went to work had to work in a quarry and carry rocks for some building purpose. There were also manufacturing plants and industries in and around the camp. The fact that they did not designate us for work and placed us in the political section of the camp meant that we would not stay in that camp for much longer. They did take us to work a couple of times to carry rocks back and forth just to keep us busy.

Buchenwald was not quite paradise, but for us it was a relatively comfortable and short-term transit camp. The food was reasonable, there was enough bread and soup – which did not mean that we were not hungry – but at least we did not have to work constantly. We could rest a little, a respite we badly needed. For a short while, we did not suffer from bugs and lice. After ten days, we were notified that in the morning after formation we would leave Buchenwald, and so, the next day, we were forced to board cattle trains. There was fresh and clean straw on the wagon floor. I will never forget the day we left, the constant calling of numbers over the loudspeakers... They called numbers throughout the ten days, but we were not candidates for selection since we were in transit. It turned out that we were on our way to Schlieben, a branch of Buchenwald. It is possible that Schlieben appears in archives as Buchenwald Number X. The same is true of Flossberg.

It is incredible how the educated German people invented ways to wipe human beings off the face of the earth. They read numbers over loudspeakers and people had no option but to report to their own death. Very few people managed to flee from Buchenwald, and these were generally Germans. In Buchenwald were German political prisoners from many countries that were conquered and occupied, especially France, Holland and Belgium, and of course Germans who were unwilling to cooperate with the murderous regime. They saw themselves as Germany's future leaders.

We boarded the train, 60 to 80 people per wagon. Once again, we were headed towards the unknown.

The transport from Buchenwald to Schlieben was short and took place in an open cattle car, which was highly unusual for the Germans who were used to packing 120 per locked wagon.

There was no food or water. Like in the transport to Buchenwald, it was slow with many stops on the way. Priority was always given to military and civilian trains, so our transport was crawling along very slowly. They were not in a hurry. Older SS men were guarding us, telling us they would shoot if we tried to escape.

Part of my group had stayed behind, including those who had held positions of trust at Skarzysko and the weak and sick. We were not sorry to leave this awful place where numbers were constantly called over loudspeakers. Never again did I see a single person alive from the transport that had taken me to Buchenwald.

After a few hours we arrived at a train station named Schlieben. We were ordered to step down and march up a hill towards a camp adjacent to a plant manufacturing anti-tank weapons called Panzerfaust. These consisted of a pipe and an explosive head and were very easy to use. The Germans needed the weapons badly; they also distributed them to the civilian population so they could defend themselves against enemy tanks. Enemies were quickly advancing towards Germany's borders from every direction.

It was the summer of 1944. The camp had not yet been built but there was an area enclosed with double, non-electric barbed wire. There was a shack serving as a kitchen for the very small population, shaven French women, and a large stack of barrack wood on the ground waiting to be erected.

We entered the camp area, stood to attention, and were asked who among us was a carpenter, construction worker, electrician, locksmith and so forth. Once suitable people had been identified, they were given tools and set to work. The rest of us had to clean the surrounding area, which was neglected.

The first night we spent outside, on the building material. The next day, some of us were sent to the plant to work. However, the people there were not ready to receive us as the plant was still unfinished. They put me in a group that was responsible for installing railroad tracks; others joined teams that had to clean up the yard, guard posts, offices and roads. After a few days, the area started resembling a functioning plant and camp. The barracks had been erected, though there were no beds and no heating; no basic infrastructure serving human needs. Nothing.

At night, we would sleep on the concrete floor. We were cold, and people started getting sick and dying. Even when we found a furnace, we had no means of utilizing it. In Skarzysko, there had been an iron furnace, and sometimes we had managed to get coal from the electric plant. In Buchenwald we had had our uniforms, but here we lacked clothing – we had no underwear whatsoever. We could only take cold showers, but even that was difficult to accomplish. We got little food, could not cook, and the local population totally ignored us.

More and more transports arrived. They included Russians, Poles and prisoners of war. This was the first time that I was in a mixed camp, not just a Jewish labor camp. Schlieben contained about 2,500 to 3,000 people, half of whom I estimate were Jewish. More Jews would arrive, but the number of residents in the camp never increased. At this point, no one cared anymore as to who was Jewish and who was not. Although there were some Russian soldiers, most of the camp's population was civilian. There were no politicians here; they were incarcerated in camps like Buchenwald and Mauthausen.

When the plant was ready for production, the prisoners were organized into work teams and departments. At that time, there was only a 12-hour day shift. HASAG owned this plant too. We were guarded by older SS men, long-term members of the Nazi party. One of them even apologized occasionally and said he was sorry for what he was doing. He said he preferred staying home and playing with his grandchildren, and tried to console us by saying the war would end soon and that we would return home. Home?

Security at the plant was relatively relaxed, but in the camp, young SS men were the guards and would beat and abuse us.

One day, a transport arrived from Hungary. The people were wearing Hungarian military uniforms, not one of them spoke any language other than Hungarian, and they looked physically very healthy. Later on, they related to us that they had been recruited into the Hungarian military, that they were all Jews and that they had been sent to the Russian front. They disliked the Russians because many of their friends had been killed. They were unable to comprehend how the Germans were about to treat them, and what tortures they would endure at their hands. They were convinced that the Germans would be nice, nicer to them at least, because they had fought for Germany. Although they had not volunteered to fight, they had fought anyway, and anyone who had shown such loyalty to the German Reich would surely be well taken care of, so they thought... That is why, they explained to us, they were not afraid of this Schlieben camp. We could not persuade them that they were slaves and prisoners. Some of them tried to conceal their Jewishness, thinking it might help. But this was a camp with many different people, and the Germans did not exactly care who was a Jew and who was not. That was a plus for us, because we were just considered inmates.

During the first few days in Schlieben, a Wehrmacht officer showed up. He said he had come to run the camp. When we returned from the shift, we stood in our usual formation. This officer climbed on top of a table and encouraged us to work for the war effort. He said: "The war is almost over. Soon, you will all go back to your homes; therefore, I am asking you to make an effort and work. This situation will not last much longer." Of course, the next day this officer disappeared and was never to be seen again. This man's speech was strange for us to hear. We were no longer used to listening to someone who did not order, scream at or abuse us. He was an older man and must have known what to expect from such a regime. He used words like "request" and spoke to us with dignity, using the polite third person pronoun. I had not heard such language for a long time, and it was indeed bizarre to hear a man dressed in a German uniform address us with courtesy. We understood that something bad would happen to him. He probably finished his life in some extermination camp for addressing us like human beings.

The Hungarian group who had arrived in such good shape and thought all would be well fell like flies and were totally unable to cope with the tremendous difficulties in this small camp. To this day I do not believe that even one of them made it through alive. In any event, I never heard from anyone that any of them had managed to stay alive. Why them and not others? They were more prominent in the camp, they did not adjust, and they could not make themselves disappear among us. We were old hands and experienced at this abysmal existence, and they were easily identifiable because they only spoke Hungarian.

I was assigned to the railroad tracks. The Germans demanded high-quality work, order and rhythm. That is what they had grown accustomed to with professional German workers who knew their craft well and worked eight hours a day, enjoyed good health, and who at the end of the work day went back home to a family and plates full of good and healthy food.

We worked 12-hour shifts, we were literally starved to death, we were exhausted, we could never rest, we had torn rags on our backs and we had no shoes. We were hungry, always hungry, and were not trained or able to work like these German railroad professionals. We were also always beaten during work, and sometimes killed. We were systematically murdered in cold blood by enthusiastic assassins.

In Schlieben, as in Flossberg, there were no organized murders per se, no real implementation of the "Final Solution". Murder in these camps was not necessarily pre-planned. It was a free for all, and anyone with a weapon killed, without permission from anyone. There were no selections because these camps were not prepared for large-scale genocide. They were new camps and created to meet urgent needs. Neither the Gestapo nor the SS had much control over these camps.

Hunger can perhaps be explained, but it cannot be understood. Our hunger was continual from the time Warsaw was bombed. It was also a psychological hunger because of the rations. We had to survive 24 hours a day on 150 to 200 grams of bread and a liter of watery soup at lunch. The hunger made us want to drink a lot of water to make us feel full. Sometimes the starvation made us confused, our thoughts unclear, and we concentrated our minds on food alone, we could think of nothing else. We would discuss smells – smells of meat, of bread and butter, of other foods that we could only fantasize about. We always spoke about food and how it smelled. We were constantly tired and worked by the power of momentum and not physical strength. We were propelled by the power of fear, completely lacking physical and mental strength.

In Schlieben we could not barter or trade or exchange because we were on German territory. We needed clothing and food, and some needed cigarettes, but we had none of these things. All we had was an old striped uniform and wooden shoes.

Schlieben was a concentration camp for all intents and purposes. One could not get anything beyond the ration, and on this ration alone, no one could survive. The soup we received was mainly water with some unidentifiable material floating on top. Rarely would we find a piece of meat in the soup, and if we did it was usually foul tasting and foul smelling. Even though we were starving, there were times we were unable to swallow the spoiled miniscule portion of meat. We were constantly on the verge of death by starvation. We had no strength left, and were all afraid of becoming Muselmänner.

Throughout the war, there were cases of people going insane. Most ran to the electric fences and committed suicide. Sometimes someone tried to attack a German, so they would shoot them. Some of the suicides were by hanging. It was a difficult task, because no one among us volunteered to help them die. They could not stand the hunger and suffering anymore, but usually the Ukrainians and Germans would get there first and shoot them. If they thought someone was behaving strangely, he would be killed.

Many people stopped eating altogether. They skipped a "meal" and died. That's all it took. One missed "meal" was enough. This phenomenon was commonplace in the camp. We did not try to save these people, there was no point. If someone was saved once, they would just try again later. I know of a case of a young man who threw himself on the tracks inside the factory and the train cut off both his legs. He was miserable until he died. He received no treatment whatsoever and was in unbearable pain. Even here, suicide had to be properly planned so that no further pain would be added to the suffering.

One day, the supervisor decided that we needed to learn how German professionals worked. We had to work in the same rhythm come rain or shine. There was a lot of rain. We were wet to our protruding bones but had to work regardless the weather or our physical condition. There were no selections like in Skarzysko, but people died from hard work and the beatings joyfully given by the guards and supervisors.

The scenery was beautiful. There were forests, and from the hill we could see a lot of green vegetation and villages. The town below looked quaint and pastoral, and on Sundays we would hear the church bells. We felt that only a very short distance from us life was going on as usual, without crazy people, that there was a normal world different from our own just a few steps away. In Germany no one bothered the Germans, and their families did not know, understand or care about what was happening around them or to us. As long as the war did not directly concern them, they went on living. We felt envious of them and their plentiful lives. We were dying by the thousands, by the millions, from starvation, murder and exhaustion. And they lived life as if nothing could touch them.

When their turn came and the war affected them too, I was already far away. The American bombings also hurt us. They bombed German food warehouses and railroad tracks and in consequence the Germans gave us even less food. When anything German was destroyed by bombs, they would take revenge on us. In Flossberg, a bomb took the roof off our barrack and snow fell on our faces and bodies as we laid there, ready to die.

A few months went by. We continued installing and repairing railroad tracks in the plant and around it, and one day my group was transferred inside the plant to carry anti-tank weapons, the Panzerfaust, from the department which was building them to the location where they were filled with explosives. At that time work in the camp had been completed, and other types of tasks had been accomplished as well. The tracks were in place, the camp was organized. They left a maintenance crew and brought some more transports from Buchenwald. The camp was full, harboring about 3,000 prisoners. It was then that we started to work in two 12-hour shifts, day and night.

There was no Jewish police to bother us, and we did not often see the Gestapo in the camp either. Except for the guard towers, there was no contact between our masters and ourselves. Sometimes one of them felt like fulfilling an important mission for the homeland, and for the Führer, and would call someone from beyond the fence. When the prisoner approached, the guard would shoot him; a heroic act, which he would laughingly tell his friends about at night over beer and food. He would be proud of himself, and the other guards would imitate him the next day, and they would all laugh and party and be happy with themselves. How brave and loyal they were for the Fatherland, for the Führer; this was their way of saving their country from a coming defeat.

Defeat arrived very rapidly. Retreating did not help and they took out their rage on us. The more bombing they experienced, the more of us they killed. Here there was no paradox. When they hurt us, their manpower weakened and production slowed down. By this time, there were no masses of prisoners of war anymore, nor others as a matter of fact, especially Jews. There were no Poles either as Poland had in the meantime been conquered by the Russians. The Germans lacked workers for agriculture and industry, but they still did not improve our conditions although with just a little food, they could have forced us to produce much more. They did nothing except eliminate us methodically. That is how they shot themselves in the foot.

One day, when I was on a day shift transferring Panzerfausts – which we put onto carts that were placed on rails that curved between the production points – I noticed a man sitting near a furnace. He looked like he was going to die; he seemed closer to death than life. He was sitting there crying. I felt like I knew him. I approached and asked him for his name. His crying intensified and he asked my forgiveness. He said he was the policeman who had beaten me in Skarzysko, the one who beat me so badly that I ran to an SS man and begged him to kill me – but he refused to waste a bullet. Here I was, watching this man cry. I could have killed him in an instant, nobody would have bothered to say anything, nobody would have investigated, nobody would have wondered why. Nobody would have cared. But I did not touch him.

He kept asking for my forgiveness and begged that I help him with some food, which I did not have. I do not know if I would have given him any food had I had some. He did not deserve my help for what he had done to me, but maybe if I had had some food, I would have given him some. Now I am not sure anymore. He was later dragged to formation by his team, and then he died.

I did not harbor feelings of revenge. I cried that day for our common bitter fate and harsh destiny that made him behave the way he had when he thought he had power over me. If it had not been for the war, this man would certainly have been a respected civilian in his town, but in this world the Germans created, he died like a miserable dog with no one to care about him. His family had probably already been murdered in some camp and no one will remember him kindly. This tragedy, which I lack strength and talent to describe, was man-made. It was premeditated, put together by Europe's ruling elite. It was planned by the most cultivated people of Europe, a people with a long history of tolerance towards foreigners, especially towards Jews. It was the German people who created the conditions for what happened, who initiated and carried out this systematic genocide. They were the same people that my parents told me would behave well because they were so educated and advanced, better than the Poles, infinitely better than the Cossacks, they said, we did not need to flee or be afraid. Everything that we heard about them could not be. This opinion still prevails in some circles today after fifty years; even I still cannot wrap my head around what the Germans did, executing millions of human beings.

But they murdered us, and they also murdered me. I stayed alive by coincidence, not because they wanted me alive, but because it so happened; maybe I was just lucky. I am not a great believer in miracles, but if it wasn't for hundreds of miracles, I would not be alive today and would not be writing my story.

Germans and servants of Germans: you like dictatorial regimes, and you committed crimes unparalleled in history – the crimes of wiping the Jews off the face of the earth and other people as well, and no one stopped you. You chose to do this degrading job. You killed without compassion, and with no excuses. Today, when you are so respected on the world stage, the world chooses to forget what you did just fifty years ago. But you murdered me and my whole family, and most of the Jews from my town, and a third of my people, and I cannot forgive you. In my eyes you will always be criminals, murderers, and all those who helped you are worth what you are. You should be ashamed for all future generations, you should be ashamed in front of the whole world, you are murderers of innocent people, of men, women, children, old people, people who never hurt you, who fought on your behalf in all your wars and who died for Germany. It was these good, loyal human beings that you sent to death camps, those who brought you so much honor, including Nobel Prize winners, who had to be afraid of you and hide. You murdered the music of Jewish composers, there is not enough paper and not enough mental and emotional strength to describe everything you did, all the harm you caused, all the pain and the suffering you brought into this world including to your own Jewish population. There are not enough tears to shed.

So little time has passed and once again you are a respectable country and people. Live with this dilemma and I hope you will never find peace and never live like normal human beings. I will never live in peace, and I hope that you will not either. I believe and I hope that the day will come when time and nature will take revenge on you Germans and your despicable servants for what you did to us between 1933 and 1945. Such a day will come.

In his book *The Rise and Fall of the Third Reich*, Shirer relates the testimonies of some Germans in the Nuremberg trials. The Germans were much more cruel than I describe. The book features just a short passage on some medical experiments, not necessarily even the worst ones. An SS officer, Josef Kramer, a veteran murderer in Auschwitz and Mauthausen, describes how at the beginning of August 1943, he received from Professor Hirt, from the Anatomical Institute of Strasbourg University, 80 prisoners to be gassed. With the help of a few SS men, they pushed the women into the gas chamber after forcing them to undress. The women stood there naked and vulnerable. They closed the doors and Sivers, one of the committed assassins who was Professor Hirt's assistant, piped in gas. They looked through the window and saw the women breathe for half a minute before they collapsed. When they opened the doors, the women were dead and covered in excrement. He testified that he repeated this procedure until the 80 women had been killed. When asked what his feelings were at that time, he said: "I did not have any feelings because I received the order to kill, and that was what I was trained to do."

According to the testimony of Sivers, Hirt continued his gruesome work by cutting off the women's heads. In September 1944, Hirt ordered the bodies to be cut up and burned. Prisoners with a tattooed number on their arm were injected with a lethal liquid and their bodies were taken to the pathological ward where they were flayed. The skins were subsequently given to Mrs. Cook who made lamp covers out of them. After that, Hirt had prisoners shot so that they would be left "intact".

These stories go on and on, there are so many horrendous atrocities committed by this "cultured" people and their antisemitic friends – Ukrainians, Slavs, Poles, etc. Their savagery, and brutality had no limits. My personal anger and pain are overshadowed by many other stories similar in their cruelty and bestiality. These were educated people, academics who with their own hands committed the most atrocious crimes, and never expressed sorrow or remorse in court for what they had done to so many people. It was the upper class who were in the dock at the Nuremberg trials, and they justified their actions by saying that as masters of the world the means justified the ends. Any type of torture and murder was legitimized and deemed acceptable and, moreover, was encouraged by their countrymen.

Not one out of the 80 million German citizens rebelled against these low-lives and even today they are a people with a leading role in international affairs and world politics. If one day another creature resembling Hitler in his philosophy and views rises to power in Germany, they will turn their back to democracy and liberalism. They will embrace him, and again, united as one, they will follow the leader and commit another genocide, no questions asked. It may be against another community, it won't necessarily be the Jews, but someone will pay the price, because in Europe there aren't millions of Jews anymore, they are already dead. Next time, the Germans will find someone else. That is their way. They still view themselves as masters of the universe and they will not give up. It is just a question of time. It is hard, almost impossible, to wrap one's head around the perception of a highly cultured and civilized people choosing to follow a murderous regime, and adopt a mentality and values that cherishes genocide, medical experiments on live human beings, on children, that is creative in ways to kill people and use their hair, skins, etc. as consumer goods. Such mentality and such values have no place in our world, and perhaps the world will understand that such was the German culture, and if kept unencumbered, future dictatorships may be the source for new tragedies and orgies of blood and death aided by allies who hold similarly distorted views and who lack determination and sound political agendas to be on the right side of history.

Let me now return to Schlieben. We got ready to march towards the camp, which wasn't far. At that point, someone decided to do a recount, and it turned out an inmate was missing. They counted us again and again. After three hours they found the missing man. He had died. He had died alone and away from us, so no one saw him take his last breath. Such things happened each and every day. We would stand in formation for hours on end in the freezing cold and wait until someone missing was found either sleeping, dead, or just lost, and then the young SS men would have fun with the poor soul. In the background, we could sense that the war was almost over, there was something in the air. The bombing increased until it became incessant. There were many air-raid alarms. Germany was being bombed and the Allied armies were advancing. It made us feel better, like we got a little revenge, but our existence was difficult as we felt the end nearing.

We missed our families more and more and we were so starved we were losing our minds from hunger. We could not think, our bodies could not function, and the accumulated exhaustion of all those years of suffering took over. We collapsed with fatigue and started thinking we could no longer go on. We wanted to die painless deaths, there was no more strength to feel the hurt. There was no point to such a life and perhaps to the life that would follow if after all we endured and managed to survive the war. The chance was still small that we would make it. Had I known what my future held, I would have found a way to end it then. But I was not a psychic and I was too young, I wanted very much to live. So I went on. I was too tired, tired from life at 23, how can that be? It came from hunger. I told my friends, "Those among you who will live, do not forget what happened here, take revenge, tell the world what they did to us." What youthful naivety! I was certain then that someone in this world really cared, we all thought someone cared, and that someone would listen to those who survived. Maybe these beliefs helped us survive, but this innocence and naivete bordered on foolishness. After the war ended, no one wanted to hear about anything.

Another formation and another march to work, the night shift this time. A few minutes beforehand, a good friend, Szachne, had come running, and in his clothes was hidden a loaf of bread that had to be concealed immediately because someone had seen him take it from the kitchen cart. We quickly helped him dispel his fears of being caught and the bread disappeared. A whole loaf of bread was not to be taken lightly. We shared it and marched off to work in a better mood. Szachne then told me that on the way to the kitchen was a big hole where animal bones were buried from the meat given to the Germans. They had thrown away the bones and covered them with lime. He said that if I thought we would not die from it, he would bring us some bones and we could wash them and have a taste of meat. Naturally, we decided to do it. In the following days, we washed some and cooked them on a fire to try and get the taste of meat by chewing the bones. If we had been caught making a fire to cook, we would have been executed. After our first chewing, the chewed bones were passed on to other prisoners and we had a feast, until Szachne was caught. He was badly beaten and from that day, there were no bones in any hole near the kitchen. They would bury them outside the camp. We kept working, my small team and I. We continued being slaves to the ruthless and brutal Germany.

One day when the shift started there was an alarm, and with it came the curfew. After a while we resumed our work and the electricity was turned on again. We worked on three carts, filling them up and pushing them along the narrow rails until the point where they had to be discharged. Then we took the carts back; sometimes they would get derailed and overturn. We would help each other as the work was very difficult, especially when the carts were filled with boxes. The rails were not in good condition, but no one cared as long as there were enough materials in the department. If there weren't enough materials, the Germans would beat and kill us.

Once, because the carts kept getting derailed, the three of us in the team would walk close to each other to hold the cart to prevent its fall. For some reason, one of the carts went off the rails, and we put it back on track. It was 2am. We had to arrive promptly and worked faster than usual, and as we got closer to the department the first cart derailed. We put it back on the tracks, and it disappeared inside the factory. We calmed down, knowing we had met the quota. Then the second cart derailed in the same spot, and we asked other prisoners to help us, but something happened, as if an invisible power was stopping us and we could not enter the department. We tried placing the second cart on the tracks but were pulled backwards and heard a terrible explosion. A rain of fire was coming down on us, which was extremely dangerous since we were surrounded by explosives. We got up and started running as far as we could from the wagon and the department and we never saw either again.

There was a succession of explosions and we ran as far as our strength – or lack thereof – permitted us. We arrived at the plant's fence and did not know what to do. Instinctively, we broke through; some guards even helped us. They looked more scared than we were. We all ran together into the fields and bunkers. Bombs continued to fall and each explosion sent us to the ground. We kept going until we arrived in the village where the farmers were running around in circles, confused and disoriented. No one knew what to do. Some entered their houses to listen to the radio, where it was reported that the area should be on alert and that a group of fighter planes was advancing to bomb Berlin. One of the planes broke out to bomb Schlieben. It was a surprise because the anti-aerial division was pursuing the planes but ignored this lone attacker. The fighter jet basically hit a population of old people, women and children as the men had all been drafted, causing damage to the civilian population and destroying our department, for which we were not sorry.

Among those who fled the camp were the old SS guards, who started organizing the prisoners, not even allowing us to have the briefest taste of freedom. They also prohibited us from picking what little food was growing in the fields. Gathering us one by one into a yard, they told the farmers we were dangerous inmates who wanted to destroy their Reich. That helped. With the farmers' concerted efforts, they collected all of us and managed to make contact with their headquarters at the camp. They encircled us and ordered us to march back. When we arrived, it was already daylight. The many dead had been gathered and taken away. There were still some small occasional explosions as we were led to the plant. We were given cleaning, repairing and maintenance chores, and my groups was sent to fix the tracks. The production crews, who now had few tools to work with, had to clean up everything while they were being harshly beaten, because of course it was our fault that the Americans had attacked the plant. We had to restore the plant to working order as rapidly as possible because the Germans needed anti-tank weapons urgently. A punishment unit was sent over to "incentivize" us. They knew how to do their jobs well, and to enjoy themselves.

Punishment units were not present in every camp. The fact that we were in a camp should have been enough punishment. I think the punishment unit was brought to Schlieben because they needed to rebuild the factory. I also think they brought these young murderers who were not too experienced and graduates of the Hitler Jugend because they had failed terribly in the Eastern part of Prussia and thousands of them had died. That was no secret. They badly needed a rest and time to reorganize. What better than entertaining themselves by killed weakened human beings whose souls and families and communities were already murdered? It could be considered a reward. This young violent gang followed us to Flossberg too.

If the explosion in Schlieben had taken place six months prior, they would have executed all the camp's prisoners because they knew well enough that the explosion was the result of an inside job and not an air raid. But many sources wanted to keep the truth secret and leave the camp and the factory, saving their own skin. That was why the Germans pretended that an air raid had destroyed our department. They needed the factory to keep operating, this unit was available, so they were introduced as the punishment unit. They were better trained for that than for combat. How proud they were to be murderers. They stayed with us until the very end, even their own. In camps where there were many Gestapo and SS men, there was no need for outside staff. The regular old guards in Schlieben were unable to serve at the various fronts, and they did not make our lives easier, but they were not as physically fit as the punishment unit. The factory was quickly rebuilt, and work proceeded.

The bunkers were not seriously damaged and could operate and the trains started to arrive again with materials after the tracks had been repaired. We unloaded the trains under the supervision of the punishment unit. They made sure we unloaded the boxes from the wagons, each box weighing 70 kilos (154 pounds), twice our own weight, and that we ran with them on our backs. With the 70 kilos on our backs, running back and forth, all the while being beaten vigorously by every Gestapo beast, more people collapsed and died. The fewer people to do it, the more difficult our job became, and the weaker we became. We, with our 35 kilos, had to keep the same running rhythm.

Long afterwards, it turned out that the explosion was due to sabotage on the part of a German director who had been a spy for the Americans; he had blown up the explosives in the department. He was a short man and wore a blue gown. After Schlieben (which was located in East Germany) was conquered, he returned to the factory wearing an American military uniform. One hundred and ten people worked there, all Jews.

All that was left of the department was a huge hole, and inside the hole parts of the train wagon. All the people had been killed and buried under the rubble. To my deep regret, my good friend Moshe Wallerstein, who had big dreams about moving to Australia with me after the war to become a millionaire, was among the dead. So close to the end, he died a tragic death. Of course, there is no tomb there. The restoration phase did not last long, and within a few weeks, measures were taken to transfer the factory somewhere else. No more trains came.

When I thought of Moshe Wallerstein, I knew there was space for sadness and mourning and grieving on the loss of a friend, or the loss of a family member. Of course, we were sorry for each loss, but someone who had spent over four years in such a hell cannot afford to be too touched by it. There was a difference between the loss of a friend and the loss of family members. Some relationships were coincidental friendships with people whom we did not really connect with, but that was not the case with Moshe Wallerstein. The bond with him was indeed coincidental, and we probably would not have connected under different circumstances. He was older than me by about ten years, and his background was completely different to mine. He had a heart of gold, but of course that was not enough to survive. He had lost his wife and child, his parents, and the rest of his family in the Warsaw ghetto. He was lonely, as was I.

I had met some people from Sochaczew who had ended up at Werk C from Majdanek, and they told me horrific details about the ghetto and my townspeople. And what they did with those who remained; their fate was clear. In any event, both Wallerstein and I understood that we had a good, warm relationship although we worked in different departments and lived in different barracks. Often we did not even see each other since I worked nights and he was always on the day shift. The year was 1943, a most difficult time in Skarzysko, with the harshest selections, and an increasing number of executions in the woods. Transports were arriving regularly, and the selections were proportional to the number of new arrivals. We needed a lot of encouragement, psychological and otherwise, in order not to break down. Therefore, our friendship came right on time. The fact that we did not see each other much only reinforced it. He saw me as a younger brother, and I considered him an older brother. We always spoke of a future which at that point I was not taking seriously. He was dreaming of being in a good financial position and saw in me a partner for a future business.

To my deep regret, this whole dream was ruined by his sudden death. For me it was a great shock and I was very sorry. Had he survived, it is possible that my life would have taken an entirely different turn. Immediately after the explosion killed him, I suffered a serious trauma, but the situation was such that I had no strength or time to mourn his death, because the punishment unit was immediately brought in and there was no spare time to cry. Conditions changed quickly, and new inspiration came because the war was almost over.

Very seldom do I remember myself without hope. Although I felt great pain when I lost Moshe, it would have also been a traumatic situation under normal circumstances. Not many people manage to have real friends. A friend like Moshe is hard to find. His loyalty had no limits, but I could not lose control and had to be strong and keep on living. I am sure that he would have told me to keep on living, and tell the world about the atrocities we had both endured. That was the only way to survive, and most people went on if they could. Some fell, some kept on living, only so that we would be there to bear witness to the horrible tragedy.

My "victory" is bitter, but I am alive to tell about the crimes, and I won over the murderers who murdered me. Unfortunately, I have to bear witness for Wallerstein too.

We started getting organized for an evacuation, because the American army was approaching so the Germans decided to close down the camp and relocate the factory.

Once again, I had to remind myself to forget my previous existence, to remember not to miss a family that was no longer, to forget loves of my childhood and adolescence, to forget all those who were no longer alive, who would never be anymore. I had to focus on what I was ordered to do in the present. I had to pull myself together, if only to survive, because if I died, there would be no one left from my whole family. The instinct of survival was strong although sometimes I wanted everything to end.

I cannot possibly put on paper everything that went through my head and everything I thought and dreamed about until I arrived in Flossberg. I still do not know how I got there, there are thousands of unanswered questions, and no one will ever know just what we had to go through. We want to tell the world but are limited by our memory and pain all these years later [this manuscript was written about 50-55 years after the war]. Somehow details seem crucial, and it is difficult to remember them all. No detail here is irrelevant or insignificant, and they will be left to historians and interpreters in the future. I would like to hope that the events will not be distorted and that the details that will be added will remain authentic and faithful to what happened to us. I would like to quote Mrs. von Staden, the German writer who says in her book:

"We, the Germans, became a people without a culture, a vulgar people without compassion and obnoxious without proportion."[4]

What more can I add to these words? Maybe one day her people will understand what Mrs. von Staden and her mother understood during the war.

Again, we stood in formation, to attention. A train was coming and we were surrounded by the Gestapo. We climbed onboard the cattle trains – we were almost used to it by now – and again we were on a transport. Where to? The question hung in the air, but as usual there was no answer. If there was ever an answer, it was accompanied by beatings to death, so it was better not to ask. The camp's veterans knew this already. Some of us were on the train like cattle, some stayed in Schlieben.

After a short ride, the train stopped and we got off in a small station close to the forest. There was not a single human being in sight, and not one sign of life besides a few barracks. What would they do with us here? Would it be like in Schlieben? Perhaps they would make us build a factory and make us work like before, and maybe, maybe, we would make it alive to the end. We could think no further than staying alive at this point. We were occupied by the idea that they would eliminate us there before the end of the war and that no one would ever know. The end could be felt and seen on the ground. A big part of Germany had been conquered by the Allied armies and the German military was present in the area; we would see divisions of the Wehrmacht.

We had now entered the second half of February 1945.

The end of the war was so near, what would be easier than to kill us? All the years we spent in camps they kept telling us that they would let no one out alive so that there would be no witnesses. Therefore, it made sense that the time had come for them to exterminate us.

We got off the train and got organized in the barracks, all empty but for rough wooden planks; there were three levels of those, and a little straw probably brought from a camp that had been eliminated. I think Italian prisoners had built this camp, because theirs was relatively close by. The straw was filled with bugs and lice, unlike in Schlieben. There, for eight months, we did not have pests after the disinfecting we went through in Buchenwald. It took just one day before we were all re-infested.

The next day a train arrived with equipment and clothing. We were sent to unload it. We decided to change our clothing and wore a few layers of the new items we had found on the train. The guards laughed when they saw us, so fat with clothes. It did not bother them, and thus we had created a window of opportunity for bartering pants for bread and some other piece of clothing for flour. Here and there someone had a cigarette too, which was extremely rare then.

The next day, another train brought prisoners and more equipment and tools, and the Germans started getting us organized to do labor. Some of the people were taken to the forest to fell trees in order to prepare the area for the establishment of a new factory. Another group was taken to drag the trees out of the forest, and others to prepare the area for the building of the plant. Other groups worked building barracks in the camp, digging latrines, arranging pipes for showers and building roads. More and more transports were arriving as well as the punishment unit of the SS men in Schlieben, the Strafkommando. When they arrived we knew what was awaiting us, and it was not a good life.

During the first day of work, I was assigned to a group which carried trees out of the forest. That was hell. Dante's inferno was a joke in comparison to what we went through. They made us carry whole trees on our shoulders. Those who were taller than the rest broke under the trees' weight and fell to the ground, then the next tallest ones fell, and then the tree would fall on all of us.

Sometimes, in order to entertain themselves, when a group was somewhat managing to carry the heavy tree on their shoulders, the monster who was guarding us would climb on top on the tree trunk. While we carried it, he would run back and forth along the trunk as he was beating us on the head and stamping on our fingers with his boots. If he fell off, he would go completely crazy and beat us savagely, kill and murder us until he calmed down. I had never seen such a sight. There were days I missed Skarzysko, and that was no paradise either.

At the end of the day we returned to a camp that had been

readied, food distribution followed, and then a long line to the toilets, basically a round wooden structure with holes on it. We were masses of exhausted, sick and starved human beings. Most suffered from diarrhea, and there was just one hole for everyone. The pressure was unbearable. Some could not help themselves anymore and had feces running down their legs. Many times people just collapsed and died as they were waiting in line to go; others died running to the hole. Those who stood in line waiting for the hole could not move, because the instant someone moved an inch, nobody would let him back into the line.

In order to keep warm, we would risk our lives by taking empty sacks of concrete. We tore them up and placed them under our clothing, and sometimes used them to light fires. That was very dangerous. We also used these scraps of dirty paper as socks and "toilet paper". If caught with any of these torn paper sacks, we would have been executed instantly. But there was no furnace, no heating, and this was smack in the middle of winter. In the morning, during washing, you had to take your clothes off and put them aside, and when you were finished, your clothes would have been stolen. That was a very serious issue. Although the bugs and lice were eating us alive, we strove to keep as clean as possible.

But it was dirty all around us, and the work was excruciatingly difficult, the food horrendous and the portions too tiny to survive on. We started seeing many people closer to death than life – the Muselmänner – and we listened to their sighing and saw that they were unable to get up and go to work. To the extent that such a person can speak or think, they always imagined us eating and always smelled nonexistent food; they always thought food was being distributed when it was not, and they always thought they were being deprived of food while others were not, which was not the case, because we were all starving. We, too, spoke only about food, but they would imagine food where there was none and did not hear us anymore. And then their souls left them. First by dozens each day, then by the hundreds.

The transports kept coming but the camp population decreased. Here we had no gas chambers nor crematoria, but so many died each and every day that no new transports could make up for the losses. People died en masse. Those who could not eat, who were unable to get more than the tiny ration we received, had no chance of survival.

In Flossberg, luck and camp experience played an important role for senior slaves. There were Russians, Poles but mostly Jews, and we would trade with cigarette butts and potato peels. We would barter with the Italian POWs who had no clothing and get some food in exchange. Some, despite thorough searches, had managed to hide their gold teeth. Their turn would come, and they would have to trade them in the Flossberg camp. We found many ways to take their teeth out and sell them for a ration or two of bread or some cigarettes. For many of the Russians, smoking was more important than eating, and they would barter with food. Once I saw Russians cut a piece of human flesh from a corpse, a little bit of meat from the person's buttocks and eat it raw. It did not help them survive.

While there was violence against us, Jews rarely acted criminally against one another in the camps. There was some food stealing, or stealing a piece of rag, but unlike the Russians and the Poles who would occasionally murder one another, there was no violence among Jews. Some had clothing in addition to the striped uniform, and they would barter, anything to get something to swallow and keep existing. Sometimes, someone would barter for a bone or some meat from an animal, sometimes a whole slice of bread or one whole potato. Some sold their last piece of bread for a piece of cigarette, even just the end of it, knowing that they would die the next day because they would have no physical strength to stand in line for food, for the "soup" we would get. I understood those people. There was no desire to live despite nearing end.

I, too, was too fatigued and too tired to want anything, and that was a dangerous stage, because there were mountains of dead people each morning during formation, and the trains would not cease to arrive, carrying equipment and battered, shattered, broken shadows of human beings. Some came from concentration and death camps, some were really experienced in this type of existence, and some, like me, managed to go on for yet another day. At night, we would only dream of food, our hunger had no boundaries, we were hungry every moment of every day. We started seeing sores on every part of our bodies, but, of course, there were no bandages. I had not even been fantasizing about medication for the past few years. Our state was worsening and there was nothing we could do. Skarzysko and Schlieben and Flossberg, all corporation-owned. How ironic.

One day I was sent to unload a wagon and came back with a fortune – a few layers of clothing. All of a sudden, I was Rockefeller. I had something to sell, but I no longer knew how to do it. Inside the wagon where I was working, I saw names and addresses scratched into the wall by the many people who had been transported in that wagon. There were names of Jews, Russians and Poles, and they told their bitter fate on the road to death.

How did the Germans, while being defeated in the war, still have so many trains to carry rotten barracks with filthy straw that no one needed anymore? And transporting human beings with one foot in the grave? Sometimes they were thrown away immediately upon arrival, sometimes with items that no one needed. They would drag diseased, exhausted skeletons of human beings from place to place; many of them were dead on arrival. They did everything to exploit us to the maximum. It is astonishing to me and I do not understand it, even a veteran like myself, after so many years, I am unable to figure out how they managed to run a whole network, and use so many people for its maintenance when there was no point to it whatsoever.

All this was done simply to exterminate human beings, people totally innocent of any crime. Even if it caused them to lose the war, they did not stop, they continued to kill and murder to the bitter end. In the meantime, Wehrmacht soldiers were in the area and started organizing anti-aircraft defense as well as ground defense. Their vehicles were being operated on coal which consisted of small cubes of dense processed material that was somewhat soft. In a short time, these cubes of coal became food for us. People would chew it and, surprisingly, if they had diarrhea, it would stop. But many fell sick. Others would cover the coal cubes in grease or engine oil, but that caused them to die faster instead of surviving longer.

The Wehrmacht seemed like a shadow of an army; it was not what we had known it to be. The soldiers were spreading out in the forest. We understood that this army was no longer capable of opposing the military pressure mounting against them, but we did not understand why they did not surrender. They had no chance, how could such a deplorable army confront the Allied forces? But they did not give up, they fought to the end. They were sure – and they were right – that Hitler and Nazism were the bible of the great majority of the German people, and they continued to fight for what they believed in. Even those who opposed it until 1933 supported Nazism voluntarily, exactly like the Austrians did. They wanted the 1938 Anschluss and were proud of their Austrian product, Hitler, their despicable murderer – they admired and adored him. Those who joined the party behaved more cruelly than Germans who did not join, but they all took part and helped. Except for some rare examples, they all worked towards a Nazi victory.

One day my team was ordered to work on the tracks. We got organized into a group of ten people, all Schlieben "graduates". We started doing the usual work and an SS man joined in guarding and supervising us. His name was Becker. He was a bit younger than me, resided somewhere near the camp, and was a product of the Hitler Jugend. We had to address him as Herr Rottenführer.

We started installing new train tracks and repairing old tracks, and sometimes other work groups joined us. Most of the time the work was done far from the camp. The problem was that this Becker character was known to be a murderer. Each day, before he left for work, he would join some group and when they started working, he would find a victim and assassinate him. In general, it was a Russian, but sometimes it was a Pole. Not that he refused to kill Jews, of course. Each morning as we were leaving for work, we were left unguarded and he would turn up later, after he had killed someone. My relationship with him was relatively good. We were "acquainted". He knew all of us and called us by our names, but that did not prevent him from killing.

One day, he turned to me and asked: "Say Scheinwald, I think your name is German, no?" I was surprised by the question, and muttered some answer about my parents, inventing something quickly about a mixed marriage, not contradicting his theory. He accepted what I said and thought I was at least half German.

From that day on, I was considered worthy of certain rights, and there was a connection between us. He would invite me to sit down with him, and he shared his problems with me. He complained of not having cigarettes to smoke. He said that he too had problems, not just us. I suggested to him that there was a way to get tobacco. If Becker decided that someone excelled at his work, he would give him a piece of paper that he could take to the warehouse and get some tobacco.

I do not know why the Germans did not have enough cigarettes. I suppose things were starting to become chaotic. We would sell the tobacco for clothing. The clothing we would sell to the Italians for food. This is how the group became an "excellent" group, and briefly thereafter at the end of every week, each one of us received tobacco from the warehouse. Half of it went to Herr Becker, and we always found uses for the other half. We were now considered "wealthy" in the camp.

A big advantage that I had was speaking German, which the Russians and the Poles did not. Some Jews did not speak German either. Being able to speak German was critical; it was imperative that you understood what was said to you. Sometimes we were asked questions and had to give answers. If we did not understand the question and there was no answer, or if the answer was inappropriate, we were beaten to death.

The ability to speak German often saved me. I cannot say that life was boring in Flossberg. Each day was different. Each day something new happened. Each day trains arrived with equipment and new people to fill the ranks for the dead. The barracks that had been brought in were rotting, and there was no need for them because there were more dead than live humans and plenty of space in the existing barracks. Air raids started.

The forests around us were so beautiful, it was a shame our situation was so sad and our lives completely devastated, and that we were so wasted. We could have enjoyed the forest, enjoyed the tranquility and the excellent air, but now it was filled with German soldiers. They were preparing themselves for their last fight. There were Italian and other camps around us, and also some civilian settlement, but we could not physically see the Italians' camp. They did not show their faces. Maybe they should have paid some attention to what was going on in Flossberg; why weren't they doing anything?

Although my situation was slightly improved, as was my team's, I was still exhausted and starved. I did manage to get some food, even bread, for the tobacco, but the formations never ended; sometimes they lasted hours on end. I had to stand in lines for hours to wash, and then my clothes would be stolen; I would wake up earlier than everyone else to prevent that happening. By waking up earlier, I endangered my life, because one could not be awake before we were permitted to get up and go to the toilets and wash. This was extra dangerous for me since the head of my barrack was a very violent man, a German who had come to the camp for the pure purpose of killing, and who loved his job. He killed many people and no one ever stopped him. He was the Blockältester. The Germans had sentenced him to life because he was a homosexual. When we were "liberated", he was immediately arrested.

Despite the danger, I would wake up early, go to the latrine, where there were few people in line, then shower in the cold with cold water. When the camp woke up, I was ready. In

Flossberg, I managed to spend very little of my time standing in line.

The bombing raids continued. They made the guards angrier and angrier, and they took out their rage on us. They wanted revenge for the destruction that was caused by enemy fighter jets, and as usual we paid the price. The Germans claim some of the bomb raids against them were unnecessary because Germany was about to give up and capitulate. It was their opinion that raiding Dresden, for example, was uncalled for and unnecessary. What nerve.

When their turn came and the cities of Germany were bombed, they suddenly became martyrs. Dresden became a historical town where a lot of art was destroyed. The murder of six million Jews, two million Poles, and who knows how many millions of Russians and others, was that also uncalled for and unnecessary to the Germans?

The bombings allowed us to take more breaks from work. We worked, then we had to stop, waiting for the alert to be over and for the planes to leave. Sometimes planes arrived without any alarms going off and the whole area would be destroyed, although the camp itself remained intact. One time, a bomb fell into a big lake. It turned out that the lake was filled with hazardous materials. Everything started burning, and for days a thick smoke covered the whole area.

The relationship we had managed to forge with the neighboring Italian camp, whose inmates were free to wander around, benefited us. The Germans treated them relatively well, and their trade with us represented no danger to them. Besides our bartering, we could hear some good words from normal people who had more freedoms than we did, and more knowledge about what was going on, especially in the surrounding areas. They were very nice to us, and we tried to reciprocate as best as we could. They were guarded by the Wehrmacht, not the Gestapo, and they were treated as prisoners of war, which is why they received better food and certain rights.

There was no comparison with our conditions. They did not hesitate to express themselves openly, without fear of repercussions, when we were afraid to even listen to them when our guards watched us, including my "friend" Rottenführer Becker. We managed to get fresh news relating to the Russian front which was very close, and about the Germans' defeats on the Western front. These words strengthened us and gave us energy to endure the suffering, despite the harsh winter.

There was a thick blanket of ice around the barracks. The pipes kept bursting at these sub-freezing temperatures and there was no water to wash with. If there was water, it was freezing cold. The roads between the barracks and the showers and the barracks and the toilets were like walking on a sheet of ice; we wore wooden shoes without socks. We could not use the latrine because it was inaccessible and we were too weak to walk on the slippery ice.

Inside the barracks the straw had become like crumbs, everything was filthy, and the bugs were eating what was left of us. At night we climbed onto the wooden bunks, placing our clothing and shoes under our head so that no one would steal them. The Muselmänner stood in line and talked to themselves and daydreamed, half dead, urine and feces dripping down their frail skeletal bodies. The sick could not hold back either, and there was nothing to wash off the dirt with, a challenging and painful situation in itself. Under these conditions there was a great danger of an epidemic, but not during winter. What would happen when the snow melted? No one could think that far ahead.

At least there were no selections here, no gas chambers and no crematoria. There was no need for them, people died anyway. With so many dead, where would we bury them? Only the strong survived. This was a very cruel "natural" selection. And these were working people, people needed for labor, every day there were transports bringing in new human beings, and the Germans continued with their ignoble deeds, their contemptible purpose: to kill us. Most of those who arrived disappeared within a few days. The majority were Russians from other camps. Those who survived a couple of days become fewer and farther between. We were altogether about 2,500 human beings, a number that met a quota for the Germans.

When the camp was dismantled, this was also the number of people who boarded yet another transport. In this hell, the German love for order continued to prevail. We still stood to attention while more and more people fainted from fatigue and malnutrition. Many of us were envious of them because their suffering was over. The wind blew and the cold cut through our skin and it was unbearable. We shivered, and I felt that I could not bear it anymore. If this standing to attention continued, I too would fall, how can we stand for two hours in these conditions after our shift has ended? We were still standing, and the Germans were still unable to count us. When their numbers matched, they would still not let us go. Again, something was wrong. Each German had a different figure, and if someone died in the middle, they started counting all over again. We stood for hours and hours, endless hours, as they kept counting us again, again, again, again, endlessly. We continued falling and dying and they continued counting.

The same scene took place in the morning before marching off to work and at night, prior to bread and soup distribution. The assemblies never disrupted the work hours – any time lost counting us cut into our rest. When this torture was over and we stood in line for food, they started rushing the process because they, the Germans, were tired.

A kapo or his deputy would give us one unsliced loaf of bread for eight prisoners/slaves. They counted eight people passing the distribution point without getting bread, then they would give another loaf to the following group of eight people. The last person in line would end up receiving a whole loaf of bread. This created chaos. We were forbidden to have knives, and even if someone had some item vaguely resembling a knife, they would not dare use it or show it to anyone lest the Germans find out. It sure represented a big threat to the Nazi empire, so that person would be executed immediately.

In those days, we ended up eating just a crumb of bread, and even that was preceded by great pains and anxiety and beatings, and the bread would fall apart having been broken in two, then four, then eight. The barrack supervisors and the guards stood to the side and enjoyed the show, laughing at the entertainment they had staged. What a joke, what a funny show – they loved it.

No one cared. If we got sick, there was no infirmary. It was labor or death. We were now in March and rain fell constantly. We still stood to attention for hours on end, with rain dripping down our necks and our bodies shivering with every drop. The few clothes we had were soaked and we were cold. It was cold, and windy. Many people contracted colds, and the next day they could not get up for work. Since everyone had to be present at formation, people were dragged there by their friends. After assembly they could register to stay a maximum of two days in the barracks. Then they could go to see a "doctor" who may permit them to stay in the camp. After the permit expired, they had to go to work and in most cases, they did not make it back to the camp. There was always an available murderer who would gladly help them to die.

This is how I existed for two months in Flossberg.

One day I was ordered, along with some other prisoners, to unload a train, and again we managed to put on additional clothing as we were emptying the carriages, which had arrived from a death camp. We returned to work "fatter" and knew there would be food the next day. There was no logic to what was happening. There had already been an order issued to eliminate all the camps and leave no signs of genocide.

We contacted the Italian POWs and with the help of Rottenführer Becker and others, and together with my friend Szachne, we succeeded in making a deal. We returned "thinner" by leaving them all the clothing from the train in exchange for two loaves of bread for each of us, and 20 potatoes, left over from after Becker had received his share. He was not ashamed to take food from us. Until today, my conscience bothers me about the fact that I alone ate the two loaves and many of the potatoes. It was the first time in the camps I had had so much food. In truth, I was afraid to bring it back to the camp because I knew it would be forcefully taken away from me. Therefore, I decided to eat the food in the work area instead of losing it all. With Becker's approval, I buried the rest of the potatoes near a tree trunk so I would have something to eat the following day.

However, I never got a chance to eat because we were moved the following day.

The camp was woken up earlier than usual for assembly. After the counting and the standing, and the filling in of forms and another counting, we were not divided in groups but the whole camp was led to a small train station. The station was adjacent to the camp, near the tracks that we ourselves had installed and connected to the main tracks. A train with 35 to 40 wagons was already there. The doors opened and we were ordered onto the train. These were freight trains and they packed us 110 people to a wagon. A few hundred people were ordered to load the train with various equipment. Part of the train was dedicated to the camp's staff, including guards. The camp itself was not dismantled, but the equipment that could be moved was. After a few hours, the barrack heads or their delegates counted us and they locked the doors. We were in darkness once again. It was the middle of April 1945.

From the day I arrived at Flossberg until the transport, two months went by. Flossberg was a secondary camp and everyone knew the war was nearing the end. The Germans knew it, but HASAG still wanted to believe that negotiations with Western countries were taking place, leading to the creation of a bloc that would attack the Russians together in order to destroy communism. The owners of HASAG wanted to build a larger factory to meet the needs of that alleged bloc. They knew it was a dream but did not give it up until the last minute.

There was a certain degree of chaos, the management was local as were the orders, but no one took initiatives of their own except to kill. Maybe there was no central management anymore. There were many such small camps. The difference between Flossberg and the rest was that it was new and disorganized, we had to do everything from scratch and the local supervision was not trained in the management and building of a camp without supplies, not just food, but also machinery, equipment, parts, and so forth.

I cannot exactly evaluate if the description of Flossberg is complete, the more I write about it, the more I feel there are still many things that remain untold. I do not know if it is because they are too violent and vile and cruel, or because I have forgotten them with time. How can one remember so much pain for so many years? This is true for all the camps I was in. The more I add to this story, the more I feel it is not complete, and that large parts are missing, and I can only ask for the reader's forgiveness.

The train started moving very slowly. It stood idly more than it moved. That worried us tremendously, it reminded us of the stories we had heard from the death camps. The trains going there would go and stop and go and stop for days, and inside the wagons the human dazed, skeletal cargo would die of starvation and thirst.

The stop and go situation angered and scared us. We knew we were heading to our end, the question was what it would be. Would we get to see our murderers forced to put their weapons down and their arms up? As the train was stalling, going, stalling, stopping, going, we did not realize – how could we? – that the slower the train advanced, and the more it stopped, the better chance we had to survive. Here was another paradox. Each day more people died in the cattle wagons, but the more time went by, the better chance we had to arrive at a camp when the war would be over.

If we arrived at a camp prior to the end of the war, and they still had time, they would surely exterminate us. On one hand it was like an opposite race against the clock and on the other hand, we did not know how to continue existing on the train and be alive when the doors would eventually open. This is how the days went by. We received no water, and no food. When we were forced onto the wagons, Szachne, my friend, and I made every effort to stand close to the tiny opening at the top corner of the wagon. It was covered with barbed wire, but we had to make sure to be near it so we would have some air. Both Szachne and I had a pack of tobacco, which we knew the Germans wanted. They had installed on each wagon a small post on top of the roof to guard the train and make sure no one escaped. Throughout the trip they also practiced their aim, shooting randomly into the wagon to see how many people they would hit with their bullets. I assumed Becker was guarding on the roof, but I never saw him again.

With our chutzpah, Szachne and I yelled out through the vent to the guard to ask him if he wanted some cigarettes. He said: "Yes, but you must give me all the cigarettes quickly or I will shoot you." Then he shot through the roof. Knowing he could not enter into the wagon, we said no, we had nothing to lose. We said we would give him cigarettes in exchange for water and bread. He replied that he had no bread but that he had sugar and water, and that he would exchange it with us when we reached a station.

We proceeded to negotiate and agreed he would hand us the sugar and water and simultaneously we would hand him cigarettes. One hand came down with sugar, another up with tobacco. We had packed the tobacco in paper from concrete bags back in Flossberg and had hidden it on our frail bodies. The guard kept his promise and gave us water too. This bartering went on for a while and we kept on eating sugar. We filled our pants with the sugar we had decided to save and tied them around our ankles with a rope so the sugar would not fall out. We also kept some tobacco for the rest of the way. When we arrived at our destination we still had sugar in our pants. While sugar is an edible product, it does not stop the hunger and the body needs a lot of liquid to counter the sugar. We had no liquid, no more water, nothing. I felt pity for the people on the cattle train with me. But I was helpless, as were they. We were surrounded by skeletons, undernourished human beings, and we swallowed sugar and choked on it for lack of water.

On the third day, the train stopped and after a few minutes they threw three barrels of food into the wagon. We fell on the barrels. When we opened them, a foul smell emerged; the food was rotten, it has turned sour and impossible to eat. People still tried swallowing it. They started vomiting and died immediately or after a few minutes. It later turned out that the Germans had not wanted to stop the trains in order to give us food so that the Russians would not catch up with them. That was supposedly why they gave us no food the previous days.

We received the order to throw the cadavers outside, which we did, as they threatened to shoot us if we didn't. There were many dead. Now there was more space on the train, but when the Germans realized that, and found out some people could not get up and stand on their own two feet, they did not hesitate and shot them inside the wagon. After they had assassinated the people on the train, they used the time to murder a few others who were also then thrown out. They brought in a group of prisoners equal in number to those killed and added them to the wagons, so that our illusion of more space and air quickly dissipated. Once again, we were cramped and unable to move. The empty wagons were disconnected from the train, and from that day on, the same scenes took place each morning. They would refill the wagons with people from other wagons and disconnect the emptied cars. We knew how many had been murdered, and how many were still barely alive, and that the locomotive was pulling fewer and fewer wagons. Still we did not know where it was going with its miserable, starved, weak, sad human cargo.

It was a spring day, between April 10th and 15th, 1945. We could hear air raids along the way, and at night we could hear the artillery well. The train would stop during the days and at nights it would crawl, then stop, then crawl again, stopping more than moving. What we did not know then was that it was going along a narrow corridor of a few tens of kilometers between the warring armies.

On the day we boarded the train, there were 2,500 of us. The ride was endless, and we were sure we would all die before reaching our destination, whatever it was. That seemed to be the purpose. We learned later that 90% of those transported had died or been killed on the way.

At that point we thought that half of the 2,500 were still alive. What we had yet to learn was that we were not even halfway through this death ride. We were hoping we would be liberated while still on the train – we were certain that the liberating armies were closing in on us from all sides. We could hear the shooting clearly, especially at night.

One night, a group from one wagon managed to escape through the floor of the train. When the Germans realized what had happened, they immediately stopped the train, shot everyone in that wagon, and started searching for the escapees. After a few hours they caught the whole group, brought them back, made them stand on a hill in front of the tracks, opened all the train doors for us to see, and opened fire. They then picked a small group of people to dig a hole and bury them. I should add that this was done on Slovakian land. Slovakia was then an independent country that cooperated with the Nazis.

The doors were closed again and the journey continued. Time was crawling by like the train. When we stopped again, we saw from the small vent that we were in a valley. Alongside the tracks was a narrow stream of water. We wanted to jump in and drink it, we were all dehydrated. There were quiet forests around us. It seemed they had simply abandoned us on some side track, leaving us there to rot. The silence was deafening.

Then, all of a sudden, we heard banging on the doors and screaming. "Is the group that installed the tracks here?! Is the Gleisbaukommando here?"

A great fear fell upon us.

The whole group was in my wagon, ten people altogether. We thought they were going to eliminate the whole transport. We answered that we were present and trembled with fear. The doors opened and one of the guards ordered us off the train. We climbed down; one of the young men jumped and died on the spot. Perhaps he had a stroke or heart attack from fear. Thus there were nine of us, but that was just fine with the guard. We realized only one person was guarding us. If they were to kill us, more would have arrived. The guard told us he was taking us to work, but how could we trust any of them?

We walked in front of him filled with mistrust and terror, getting farther and farther from the train whose other doors remained locked. We were accompanied by this guard only, and after a while we arrived at what seemed like an old train station. It was completely destroyed. The sun was starting to appear between the clouds and we were happy to see these ruins. We had been sitting like animals in locked cattle wagons. We understood why the train had stopped. There was no way to continue, all the tracks had been destroyed and covered in rubble. A locomotive stood on a side track, obstructing the way, so that the only option was to put it back on track or remove it. And this they expected us skeletons to do.

A locomotive weighs around 60 tons and they brought us here, nine people, each weighing no more than 60-70 pounds, expecting us to put it back on track with our bare hands. There were no tools, we had no experience of this kind of work, and we wasted as much time as we could, hoping some Allied army would show up, maybe the Russians, whom we believed were close by. That did not happen, but in the meantime we were wandering "freely" around the ruins of the station looking for food and water. Then someone spotted a train driver calmly sitting and eating his breakfast.

Two very hungry young men fell upon him and took the food. The man got scared and fled, leaving his bag. Shortly thereafter a young woman arrived and started negotiating with the German guard, and later a man joined her. We had no idea what they were discussing, but we hoped for some good outcome. The important thing was that the tracks were blocked. When the young couple left about half an hour later, carts arrived with food and cigarettes that they first gave to the German and then to us, and finally to the other people on the train. They gave food to the whole transport, bringing it on horse-drawn carts. There was bread, milk and sausages for the Germans, and dark bread for us. After a hard day of work, we managed to clear the tracks and returned to the train. As night fell, the train continued on its way and "life" went back to how it was before.

All of a sudden, we felt a push to get away. We could hear the roaring of the cannons and now we heard guns and it was all so close. Perhaps we should try to escape, but the area was filled with German soldiers. We had no tools, how could we break free? Besides a rusty tin and a spoon, we had nothing. We had no strength either. And if we managed to escape in Slovakia, what would they do to us? The danger was tremendous and the decision hard and complicated.

After another day of crawling along the tracks, we stopped at dusk. Once again, the dead were thrown out, but this time they left the doors open and let us go outside. We tried to get organized and attempt to cook the few potatoes some had managed to find. Somehow, we managed to light a fire in one of the tins we had, and we cooked the potatoes in their skins. It is hard to describe or imagine how people who have nothing to eat fight over thin potato peels. We cooked as a group so that we could protect our fortune, hoping it would keep us alive for another few days.

The train stopped for a whole day. We enjoyed the fresh air. At night, we were shoved onto the wagons again. The wagon walls were scribbled with messages. All those who had scratched on the wooden walls begged for revenge. In their utter naivety, those who were transported on this train prior to us asked on the walls that we tell the world what was happening to our people. "All those who survive must tell what the Germans did to us." It was written in Yiddish, in Polish, in Russian. They begged us to tell the world about our tragedy, but no one understood that there was no one to tell because no one wanted or wants to hear.

We were innocent and thought the world would be better one day. Revenge? How does one carry out that? Who will allow us to do that? We had placed so much hope in that the "world" would save us, but it did not. The world was in a hurry to restore Germany as quickly as possible after the war. And us? What about us? We were rotting in camps during and after the war. After the war they were open camps, but camps nonetheless. For us, no one had time, interest or money, and the Marshall Plan was not aimed at us. It was aimed at putting Europe back on its feet, not human beings back on theirs. Human beings whose lives the Germans had ruined.

In the meantime, we were attempting to live, to save our lives by our own power, but that was very difficult. But we kept going with all our strength, because we were on the edge, and everything could end at any moment now. But it did not seem to end.

I sat in the corner of the wagon by myself, trying to fall asleep. I started thinking about my home and my family. I missed them, and in my mind I saw my short life pass by. I was just a boy when the war started, and here I was now. The end was so near yet I felt so wasted. I couldn't take it anymore. Here was my father, standing on the roof of the two-storied house, the house neighboring ours in Sochaczew. He called to me, telling me to take the wooden stairs up to the roof where he was waiting for me, his arms stretched out to grab me. I started climbing but the steps give way under my feet, they are rotten, and only with great difficulty, straining all my muscles, do I get closer to the top. Father managed to take hold of my hand, and with our combined strength, I reached the roof as the last step crumbled under my feet. I tried to hug Father but just as I put my arms around him, I woke up.

I sweated but before I could remember where I was I dozed off again. I saw all my family members and could hear my mother begging me to flee the Warsaw ghetto. She promised that if I followed her advice, I would survive the war. I saw Hersh during our final separation, before heading to the camp and the unknown, and he told me he wished a wandering bullet would hit him in the head so that he wouldn't have to suffer anymore. I had no more energy left for suffering this great pain, and seeing Father in his pain. We were totally helpless. Hersh, only 24 years old, was already tired of life. In my head I saw my other brothers and sisters, my uncles and aunts, my cousins, and as I was semi-sleeping, I asked myself, where are they now? Where are they?

I woke up and understood that it was just a dream. I told my friends on the train, and they encouraged me and told me that I would probably live. It was a sign from Father, they said, he came to tell you that you will make it, so it's for sure. I was completely confused by all this. When I regained full consciousness I knew where I was, and I did not feel that any future was awaiting me. I felt more and more wasted and not just from hunger. I had been on this wagon for many days and I needed to take care of my physical needs, just like everyone else, right there, standing up. It was impossible to sit, because there were 109 human beings in the wagon. We could only sit if someone died, then we would sit on them. We didn't even talk about lying down to sleep.

Night had fallen outside and it was dark. We were in the dark, literally and metaphorically. The train had stopped. Not knowing what was going on and our helplessness drove us crazy. We were doing nothing; we were hungry and thirsty. I still had some raw potatoes. It is very difficult to eat raw potatoes, but I dipped them in the sugar I still had. It tasted like death, but kept me alive although my strength was dissolving and I could barely stand on my own two feet. I felt my life was nearing its end, it would just be a matter of time before I slipped into a semi-coma and that was bad, the moment that I could not control my own body.

I was a boy again and played soccer with the other children using a ball made out of rags. And I went to the Cheider to study the Torah with the Rabbi, and the Rabbi taught me to read and write in Hebrew, and Chumash (Torah in printed form) and Rash (interpretation of Jewish philosophy and religious learning). The Rabbi did not have logical explanations, and He couldn't exactly say what god was, and he could not explain other complicated subjects either. I went to school and they taught us Polish. The Polish children teased me, there were many of them and one of me, I was alone and having a difficult time. All these images blurred into one, I heard a terrible noise and became aware of my surroundings again. The cannons were roaring at a short distance from us, and the guns rattled. The train stopped again. Some say we had been on the transport for over two weeks.

Two weeks? Could that be true? I guessed so.[5]

The next day, the train entered a small station called Mauthausen. The minute the doors opened, we understood where they had brought us, although we still could not see the camp. Just a few people came out from only two doors. There weren't even a hundred people left alive on this death transport. We were all confused and unable to function. We spun around without knowing what was going on. They gave us water and some leftover food that they had on the train. There were some civilians at the station who were openly hostile to us; hatred burned in their eyes. We learned that this transport had lasted for 17 days. That was unprecedented. They transported us for 17 days in closed cattle cars with no consideration for our needs, no food, no water, no minimal thoughts to hygiene. If it weren't for the stop in Czechoslovakia where we got off the train, not one of us would have remained alive.

This is a crime where forgiveness has no place.

They took 2,500 people, live human beings, Russians, Poles and Jews, and for 17 days held us on that transport until most were murdered, or died from starvation, disease and neglect. Is there a crime worse than that?

When we got off the train in Mauthausen, the local population could have helped us like they did in Czechoslovakia, where they brought us food and water. The Austrians did exactly the opposite. They welcomed us with hatred and rage. It was shameful and showed a lack of self-respect. They were considered a country conquered by the Nazis, and received every consideration, right and privilege of a people under Nazi occupation. There is no question about their cooperation with the Germans. From my own experience, Austrian SS men, Austrian Gestapo and even their Wehrmacht behaved much more cruelly and violently than the Germans themselves, it is no secret.

The same was true also after the war. When we asked them for help, they refused. They did not let us close to their houses nor provided help with food or a rag to clothe our naked, frail bodies. What can an individual do under such circumstances? How can one face such a situation when his fate dictates that he is lost, and no one wants to help? Every man for himself. The great suffering, this savagery, this brutality, touches one person at a time. When you fall, no one is there to help you up. Sometimes, they cannot help, but in most cases, they do not want to help. The Austrians simply refused to help.

They told us to stand to attention at the station, but it did not look like a proper formation anymore. Even the guards were tired from this difficult and long transport, but they were alive and well, healthy and robust. Just tired. It is hard to explain, and even harder to understand how even one of us remained alive. I did not understand it then, nor do I do so now. Slowly, one by one, shadows of what had once been human beings, people that were half dead, got up.

It was difficult to differentiate between the living and the dead. We all looked dead. Walking dead. After the counting, it turned out there were less than a hundred people. This line of frail bodies, this miserable group of skeletons, was then surrounded by guards holding automatic weapons and we started crawling, or marching as they called it, towards a camp called Mauthausen. The camp was high on a mountain, and we had to climb when we could barely drag our feet and our bodies were drained of energy. Skeletons, half-dead shadows, climbing up a mountain, until we reached the camp's gates. Once there, we saw the slogan invented by a gang of German murderers: *Arbeit macht Frei* (Work sets you Free).

We crossed the gate and were led to an area near the camp's kitchen, adjacent to the gas chambers and crematorium. A few people were wandering around, and told us what was going on. These people belonged to a team that was assigned to work in the showers, the gas chambers and the crematorium, and many of them had managed to survive. When we arrived, the rules in that camp were different from previously; they were now somewhat loose, but they still could not cope with the quantity of people who arrived for extermination. At that point we were all mixed, no one was asking who was a Jew anymore. The crematorium was too small to contain and burn so many corpses, even those who died of "natural causes", meaning those who had not been sent to the gas chambers. But we did not know that at that point.

We were led to an area where there was a platform on four wheels. Covering ourselves with blankets that we still had from the train, which we had taken from Flossberg, we crawled under the platform to sleep. Just before we fell asleep, we located the crematorium and the gas chambers so that we would know in which direction we would be heading when they would order us to stand in line and march there. If the line went from left to right, then we would head to the showers. If the line went from right to left, we would meet our destiny, the destiny of our friends, our relatives and our entire families.

Night fell. It was silent and cold and difficult to sleep. I was curled up inside my blanket. I thought of my bitter fate and how I had managed to get to the end, and now, at the very end, I would be sent to the gas chambers where they would murder me. Was that why I had been suffering for the last few years, all this ongoing torture for such a long time? It was sad and tragic. What a pity. What could I do? Didn't the Germans and the Austrians – who I later learned were in charge of running this camp – understand the severity of their situation? The war was ending, it was a question of days and they knew it, but they still continued to implement their "final solution", as only murderers can do. Otherwise they would have had to release all the prisoners as soon as they took command of the camp. Incidentally, not only did the Austrians take it upon themselves to run the camp, but they acted as the guards there too. All they wanted was to continue the killings, to kill as many human beings as possible, even though it was already April 29, 1945.

The war was over, but it was still going on against us, weak, sad and lonely skeletons.

Why did they continue to torture us? Why didn't they help us? German military involvement in the area was close to nil, the Austrians were occupying most of Austria and reorganizing their regime separately from Germany, but they would not budge for us. Not only did they refuse to free us, they did not even try to help, to save a few souls, those who still could be saved. Thousands could have been saved with minimal effort, with just a little food. There may have been some Germans left in the camp, but it was clearly under Austrian rule, and the whole population in the area was Austrian. They had a lot of weapons but did not lift a finger to help and continued to manage the camp as if nothing had happened and nothing was changing.

It was now May 1945. The Germans and Austrians still refused to separate themselves from the Nazi regime. They did not want to betray their Führer, he was Austrian after all, this was his homeland, he was the country's son. They refused to give up their murdering, and "Adolf Hitler, the Austrian, not the German" they said with pride. When on May 1, 1945 the fences were broken down by thousands of prisoners, innocent, unarmed, starved, sick, helpless prisoners, they did not hesitate to fire at them from the guard posts, using automatic weapons to murder thousands of us. This was a clean Austrian job; the guards of the camp would not refuse to follow the Nazi regime's order to kill us all.

But now there was no regime anymore, and we were laying down and waiting for a decision on our destiny. We lived on rumors and in the meantime thousands and thousands of new transports kept arriving, among them a transport of thousands of women who were forced to undress completely. Thousands and thousands walked around in a daze. For three days, we were lying under that platform. Three days after our arrival we received some food for the first time. They woke us up at dawn with beatings, how else, and as they were hitting us savagely, they ordered us to stand in line. Before we got up, we glanced from under the platform and although we heard the crematorium was no longer operating, we did not really want to get out. Who was still naive enough to believe anything they said?

The line was advancing from right to left, which meant we were going to the gas chambers and of course the crematorium. Our doubts increased as we advanced and received a bar of soap, a towel, half a loaf of bread and sausage and jam. We ate in seconds and remained with the soap and towel in hand. Sometimes we had received soap in previous camps, but a towel? Our fear kept increasing, this towel was proof that we were going to be gassed, that we were heading to our death. The line kept on moving. People told us that we were going to be all right, but we were dazed and looking death in the face. Maybe it would be like in Buchenwald? Maybe? Did we have another choice? Could we change anything?

I was entering a huge room. Under the ceiling was a network of water pipes, but the terrifying aspect of the room was its doors. If the doors were to close, it would terrify me. I was inside now, trembling, my body shivering from weakness and fear. I was not alone. Everyone was shaking. I heard many strange and bizarre prayers. It was a varied population from all over Europe. Each person was addressing their god in their language. The pipes thundered, but like in Buchenwald, the doors remained open and warm water started to pour.

I had not felt warm water for many months. I scrubbed my

poor, skeletal, frail body, my skin and bones. The widest, thickest part of my body was my knees. There was no flesh, no muscle. Only skin and bones. I washed myself with a lot of enjoyment and for a moment, I hoped that they would not kill us, not now. We heard rumors that later on they would take us to the mines, force us down, close the tunnels, and blow them up. We all knew they would not let us live. Now we were ordered to wash, so we did so, but what was the point of washing when we were filled with lice? We had to do what we were told, so we washed the lice, at least they would be clean. Perhaps they would have a better appetite to eat us alive. I suppose that contrary to Buchenwald, they did not have the means to disinfect us here. Things had changed from Buchenwald, eleven months earlier. The Germans were probably having some problems, maybe not getting supplies, and experiencing fear and disorder from the lack of regimented organization. But they still killed.

We were leaving the showers. There were some veteran prisoners around who knew this camp well. There were many political prisoners who tried to help, inasmuch as that was possible. The Germans could not prevent rumors. We heard a lot of them about the Germans' military condition and the general situation. It was cardinal for us to know what was going on because it encouraged us to survive. Even if we did not have food, at least we realized the Germans' defeat was near. It gave us some strength.

We also learned that a transport of Gypsies had arrived at the same time as ours, and that they were stricken with typhus and other diseases. That caused panic among the heroic Germans who decided to exterminate the Gypsies on the spot. Therefore, that day there was not enough room in the gas chambers and the crematorium, so they gave up on us and let us exist for a little while longer.

After the shower they took us to the "Russian" camp; it was a relatively newly-built camp, all the barracks were outside the fence off the main central camp. Thousands of poor prisoners were held there. They had no food; sometimes, but not often, they received a ration of soup, dirty water, occasionally a piece of bread.

We entered a very long barrack with "beds" on each side, three-storied planks. There was some straw, crumbled from overuse on the wooden platforms. It was filthy and, as usual, filled with bugs and lice. Four people had to occupy each plank in groups of two facing opposite directions. Legs between legs, feet between feet. That was true for the first two levels of the planks. I was assigned a third-level plank with Szachne, and we were forced to share it with six people, three on each side. The reason was that on the third level, there was enough space between the platform and the ceiling for one to sit up and even stand. Close to the ceiling there was a small window. If you could still stand on your own two feet, you could observe what was going on outside.

Since people died constantly, the dead were taken out every 24 hours, in the morning before the distribution of the black water they called "coffee". We had to place the dead on the floor so they could be taken away. The head of the barrack would send a work group with carts. Often people died right after the corpses were carted away in the morning; the "new" corpses stayed on the plank another day and night and we would turn the body and use it as a pillow. For a while we had more space and a dead human pillow. One more advantage to this was that we received the dead person's food ration for that day. We would say all six were alive, and no one bothered to get up and look on the plank, so whatever the "food" was, we would get it. In terms of the dead taken away in the morning, the barrack head would take their food portion, and was meticulous in counting out the rations to ensure the exact number would be distributed. Only those who "slept" on the first platform actually came down, then we would get our ration. The rest of the food was taken to the head of the barrack and distributed according to the camp hierarchy in his office.

Although we were not taken to do hard labor, we were not bored. There was action all the time; rumors were rampant. The rumor now was that the war had ended and that the SS men had fled, but then a minute later we heard the opposite.

The orchestra was still playing. The orchestra played when people went on transports or to the gas chambers, they played at hangings, and any time the Germans wanted entertainment. There was music when those in the main camp were forced to go to hard labor, including the mines. As long as the orchestra played, no one was running away.

We kept hearing we needed to stay strong and keep going at any price. This was not so simple. People dropped like flies. In our barrack, people simply fell asleep, never to wake up again. Many died on the planks and no one even noticed. I am not even speaking of the poor creatures in the central camp who went to work and carried rocks along a long road. They had to climb 170 steep steps, much steeper than standard steps, and the steps were so narrow, one could not place one's whole foot on them, but must turn it sideways in order not to tumble and fall. The rocks weighed 15 kilos (22 pounds), and along the road were kapos and SS men. They were specialists in treating the "bad elements", those opposing their regime, the prisoners here. God help him who was caught carrying a rock weighing less than 15 kilos. That person would be pushed down the stairs, and had to go back to bring an appropriately heavy rock and take it back up. In most cases, he would not reach the top alive; sometimes the fall would kill him. If he managed to make it to the top, he was beaten until he died. In the background, the orchestra played non-stop, and the crematorium could not contain the huge quantities of humans. There were mountains of corpses outside and in every corner of the Russian lower camp. Death did not stop for one second, there was no reprieve. Meanwhile, April has come and gone.

I was once asked if there were moments of happiness during this horrendous time. I was surprised by the question, and it took me a while to respond. I thought the question strange. There were indeed fleeting moments of happiness, I suppose. When warm water flowed out of the pipes in Buchenwald instead of gas. When someone got to smoke part of a cigarette. When somehow, someone managed to eat more than their meager portion. When someone accidentally met a friend or acquaintance or family member. It was a rare occurrence, but sometimes it happened. The happiest moment was when someone was almost dead and a friend – if he had one, and if that friend was still alive – promised him to remember him always and to tell the world of our tragedy. Maybe even to avenge his death. These were moments of happiness.

May 1, 1945 was a Tuesday. The sun was shining in the sky above a camp filled with breathing skeletons and dead human beings. A new month had started. There were people in Mauthausen who had lived in Eastern Europe – there were Romanians, Gypsies, Hungarians, Poles, Russians and, of course, Jews. We were all mixed and no one differentiated anymore between religions or nationalities, not even the Germans. No one cared who belonged where and why. We were all interested in one thing only: getting food, some soup, a potato, maybe a piece of bread. It was only a dream. Dreams did not come true where we existed. Was it true the war was ending? Maybe.

While "coffee" was being distributed, we heard a loud rumor: the war had ended. No one knew how or where this rumor had started. People started crawling out slowly from their bunks, others jumped and fell, some cried, some rushed out of the barrack. I got up weakly from my bunk and turned toward the window to see what was going on outside. I witnessed total chaos. People were running towards the gate. Where were they going? They were going outside, toward freedom. They started breaking open the gate. In the Russian camp, contrary to the main camp, the fence was not electric. People were cutting their hands to break it down and blood was flowing. Excitement grew and surrounded all those who could still walk. No one thought about food or anything rather than freedom. We were a huge mass of people yearning to be free.

As the fence started to come apart, with no warning, before we realized what was going on, people started falling down and I heard the firing of machine guns. From the guard posts, the guards were firing in every direction. Bullets went into the crowd and rivers of blood flowed. Some were dead, some wounded. The shooting did not cease and people still ran. It took a few minutes until we understood the tragedy unfolding in front of us. People turned back, retreated inside the barracks like beaten dogs. After the first shock, we knew hundreds had been killed and many hundreds injured. The kapos, supervisors and other management of the camp started to put the camp back in order. The only way to do that was to announce over the loudspeakers that food was being distributed. The prisoners started emerging and soon calm reigned again.

Rumors were flourishing. One of them was that Hitler was dead but that the war was not over yet. We also heard the Russian army was involved in heavy fighting inside Berlin, but that Germans still controlled many areas and continued with their killing. Inside the camp, they took the dead away, but the wounded presented a problem: how were they going to be treated? Of course, they were not. In this terrible, tragic, horrific chaos one ray of light was that the crematorium stopped working. That meant the gas chambers were not operating. Since there could not be organized killings, maybe the murders would finally end. Indeed, the situation slowly changed, except for the Austrians who continued with their constant brutal assassinations.

The Austrians would kill with no warning. It turned out these guards were not even SS men, just civilians from the area, older people who had no connection whatsoever with what was going on, people who simply enlisted to guard the camp. They received instructions and followed them with enthusiasm. They showed us how macho they were, how well they could do battle for the German Reich and their great distinguished leader, Adolf Hitler. They proved they could murder innocent people, just like the rest of the criminals.

The camp calmed down. When evening fell, it turned out that except for Szachne and me, there was no one in our bunk. The rest never returned. Some wandered outside looking for food that was not to be found. The murderers still controlled everything, and they were armed. Everyone waited for a change to happen. People were busy burying people, cleaning the camp, distributing thin soup rations. There were significantly fewer mouths to feed so the rations were bigger. There were no transports.

Saturday May 5, 1945. Shabbat. A day like the rest.

The sun rose in the sky, a beautiful spring day. I did not know what would happen that day at noon. I was lying on the third-level platform when I heard screaming from outside. I was too exhausted to look out. I remembered what had happened four days previously. I did not want to see another horrific scene like that again, so I ignored the screaming and did not move. Suddenly Szachne showed up. He was one of those who had screamed and made the noise outside. He said, "Wolf, get up quickly, come with me. Be happy. We are free."

I could not believe him. I reminded him of the massacre that had taken place a few days before. He told me to get up and look through the window. He said I would see five American tanks on the road. "More importantly," he said, "if you get up, and come out, you'll get to see what happens to the guards." That was too much of a temptation for me – I could not resist it. I dragged myself onto my feet and could indeed see the five tanks. I believed what my eyes could see, but I still could not take it in. I crawled down the platform and started walking, running, towards the gate, which was wide open. There were no guards at the posts, they had been forced down and executed. Large stretches of the fence were broken providing large openings, and yes, these were signs that this hell of mine was over.

Over? I wasn't sure. It remained to be seen.

I was naked, I had nothing on like the rest of this camp. I crawled, I ran, towards the tanks, I had to see this miracle with my own eyes and touch them. I got closer and could see the white five-cornered star. A Polish-American soldier was standing on the tank and told us that he was an American from Poland and promised in broken Polish that although the war had not ended yet, the German armies had become POWs, or were eliminated, and that there was no opposition to speak of from the Germans. "It is a question of a day or two until we'll clean Germany from all army opposition, the Americans are now in control along with the Russian, British and French forces," he added. Then he said that to his regret, they were a small division advancing before the larger armies, and that they could not help us. He thought that in a day or two representatives from different organizations would arrive and take care of us. He asked that we remain calm and orderly as much as possible until they arrived at the camp. The five tanks and the new hope then departed, leaving us with only emptiness and despair.

After the liberation from Mauthausen, we went to a mine to watch the SS men work in the very same manner that the prisoners had been ordered to do. There, I met a child dressed as an officer of the American military. The child was a 13-year-old Jewish boy. I started talking to him. He told me he had arrived at the camp with his parents, and that the camp commander had taken a liking to him. This commander was famous for his brutality and savagery but liked this boy and decided to "adopt" him. He spoilt him, gave him the title of kapo, and taught him how to torture prisoners.

One day, the camp commander decided to entertain everyone. He ordered thousands of prisoners to come out and assemble in the formation area. The orchestra was playing, and he ordered the child to hang his own parents. The child proceeded to do so. The murderers were enjoying the show and were content to see this child do what they had taught him. He was an excellent student. He told me the story matter-of-factly. Now, he applied what they had taught him by watching the guards be slaves for a brief moment. I do not know if this child is alive, or where he is. How can a person who through no fault of his own has killed his own parents function normally? I do not know. This is just one small story, there are hundreds, thousands, of similar stories. How can I remember them all... These were not out-of-the-ordinary events, these were daily happenings, this was the norm. That is why we cannot tell all of them, and that is why we must never forget.

Political prisoners, who were always busy performing public services, took matters in hand and decided to organize the camp. Here I was, free after 68 months of a savage war, 68 months, more than 2,000 days, and I was free?

This war was over, but I still did not know what the future held for me. But the day I had waited for had come. Over 2,000 days. 68 months, and I felt no joy. Why? Why?

I returned to the barrack, which was still filled with bugs and lice. I was hungry and lay down to take stock. What did I expect? Why had I fought to stay alive for so long? Was it worth it? I broke down crying and could not stop myself. There was no one there to listen to me or console me; I was alone in this world. I had no doubt that all my family members were dead, how could anyone survive such a man-made hell?

Regretfully, I was not wrong. Alone I stayed. Would I be able to go on and live? Build a new life for myself? I doubted it.

I did raise a family and I have children and grandchildren and I am happy to spend time with them, to watch the new generation. But am I happy with this life? How can a person who for 2,000 days was murdered each and every day be happy? Maybe I should divide the 2,000 days into hours and minutes.

Each minute can be divided into the innumerable dangers that it contained when I was being mentally murdered again and again. Today, I am just a body, a live body. But the rest is dead. Only by pure coincidence is my body still whole. In actuality, it was murdered a hundred times over. A thousand times over. I knew all this when I broke down and cried.

Lying on the infested platform, thoughts ran through my head like a tidal wave. I could concentrate on one detail and I fought with myself to think about what they had done to me. Only revenge was appropriate, how could it be anything else? We had to kill them too, like they killed us. Like they killed me. How could I get my revenge? As I pondered, my good friend Szachne came back with some burned potatoes. He tried to calm me down, telling me wonderful things, that the criminals, or some of them at least, had been caught, and executed as they deserved. The Russians who caught the camp's commander and his family killed them brutally.

I had no strength to get up and see the tiny fraction of revenge inflicted upon them. My hunger was nagging me, and I had diarrhea and stomach cramps and Szachne wanted me to eat those potatoes to make me feel better. Someone who had told him he was a doctor had said that coal could help with diarrhea, so I ate them and felt better. This was my freedom party. We were lost souls who did not know what to do with ourselves and saw no future on the horizon. Thoughts filled my head and I could not stop them from overwhelming me. I had been freed and yet I did not feel free. How long had it been? Where was everyone? Where were all my friends? My family? So much time had passed, and I had forgotten what a child looked like and what an old person looked like. I had not seen either for years, until I met that 13-year-old boy. I had not heard a child cry or laugh for years. During all my years in camps, I had not seen one child. That 13-year-old boy was the first child I had met since I last saw Bela, my sister, who was 7 years old back in Ozarow.

I saw an old Jew when I arrived in Italy, and some Jewish kids too. It was sad for me to watch them. This was the last vestige of the Jewish people. Millions of children and old people and youngsters and all our people were exterminated and would never return. To this day I cannot overcome the overwhelming feeling I get when I see small children and old people. That will never change.

What does a normal woman look like with regular clothes on? What does the face of a woman with a normal life look like? What does a regular house look like? With people inside, and without wars and battles? What does a house with furniture look like? With a table, and a tablecloth, and dishes and a fork and a knife and napkins? Does a house have sheets? And beds? And towels and soap and warm water too? Is there laughter in a house? And sometimes music and singing? Was there all of this that was taken away from me over 2,000 days ago? I had almost forgotten it all.

Since that day, I cannot comprehend why we are called survivors. I am not a survivor. I am a victim. What kind of survivor am I? When I read or watch TV about families murdered, or the family of a soldier who has died, it touches every home in Israel, and we are talking only about one or a handful of victims. Each victim is important, outlining the tragedy in a sharper light. I lived the tragedy of an entire people who succumbed, along with millions of others, to unspeakable terror and political exploitation. I was murdered along with everyone else and only by pure coincidence do I walk on my feet as a live tombstone. I am not a survivor, but a tragic victim of the Holocaust.

During the war years, what I learned was order and how to work in hell. I did not come out stronger, and the humiliation I felt increases with each passing day as I'm getting older, as do the feelings of longing for my lost family. Facing the profound humiliation was one of the hardest things to deal with. Not everyone was able to confront this situation. Some people committed suicide. We did not have high expectations of other peoples, but we did of the Germans, thus the humiliation was doubly painful. To this day I feel anger towards them. Until today I do not understand how they went so low, how they turned into this monster and a machine for systematic genocide. Therefore, I do not think they should ever be forgiven, and it is of utmost importance that they never forget who they are, what they did.

The world should never forgive them for the crimes they committed. If such a cultivated people can commit such atrocities, then what hope does humanity have? I do not remember completely despairing in the most severe sense of the word. Those who did, did not survive. Could not survive. Of course, with all the cruelty and evil around us, we were fearful, how could one not fear them? Only those without feelings did not fear, but I do not know if such a creature exists on earth. We lived in fear and in pity, pity not for ourselves, but for these human beings who were going through the same experiences, the Jews, the Gypsies, and, to a lesser extent, the Poles, the Russians etc. Mostly I pitied my poor people. We were in urgent need of help, but it did not come. We cannot blame ourselves for being stuck in such a situation, watching the world watch us in silence with indifference and inaction. I do blame the German murderers and the Austrians who created a death machine of such strength and who performed criminal acts of murder. Murders of babies. Children. Teenagers. Women. Men. Old people. They profited from it in every sense, they stole the arts, the money, the gold, even the golden teeth of their victims – jewelry, hair, skins – even today, their financial situation is sound in part because of this stealing.

My whole life was taken away from me during this brutal, cruel war to which I was just an innocent bystander. I simply fell victim to it. A prisoner, a slave. I was not a soldier, I did not fight, nevertheless I was stripped of my freedom for so many years, and I was humiliated in every possible way that a human being can and cannot imagine. Is this possible to understand?

I, myself, cannot comprehend the enormity of this catastrophe even though I experienced it, and it has not ended yet. Is there no end to the suffering? I know that my question is naive and rhetorical, I know that today, but after my "liberation" by the American army, I still toyed with the idea and illusions and thoughts that some sort of justice existed in the world, in this advanced world outside of Germany, I thought there was a line that a people could not cross without repercussions from the international community. Where is this world? How did it keep silent and indifferent for so long? Why was there no immediate reaction to the genocide? Why did it allow the Germans to do anything and everything that they felt like doing, anything their deformed minds and culture invented?

In 1942, after Stalingrad, and later their defeat in Africa, the Germans knew well that their end would come. Nevertheless, they continued with their systematic murders, destruction and humiliation. In one battle in Stalingrad, they lost 3,000 soldiers, and the Russian front cost them millions of soldiers – dead, wounded and POWs. Their defeat in Africa was not insignificant. Despite that, they continued to murder human beings who had nothing to do with their political ambitions. Why?

The simple answer to such a question is that only a professional murderer behaves in such a way. The hunger to kill kept motivating and feeding them and never lessened for even one moment. They neglected their war effort and used hundreds of trains, thousands of soldiers, to transport victims to extermination camps, and to transfer human beings as cargo from one camp to another. It was totally useless, fulfilling only the need to kill. At the end of the war, fifteen million foreigners were stranded in Germany and the previously occupied territories. They were all brought there as the German army was already retreating. Why else did they keep the army occupied? The trains moving forward with transports? The guards and others to handle this "job"? Was it just to save the homeland? This is precisely what they imagined. Their purpose was to destroy all those miserable weak, sad, tortured people, and to try and hide from the world their terrible crimes. They burned and buried human beings by the millions and never tired of this work and of their own boundless cruelty.

After the war we heard different and conflicting information on the number of people murdered. It is known they killed two million Poles. It is difficult to assess how many Russians, but in the millions. It is known that six million Jews were massacred. Among the six million, a million and a half were children.

Gypsies were murdered, and others from other peoples, including those who collaborated with the Nazi regime. They also killed those who managed to remain alive during the war at the very last minute. They murdered people not just physically but killed their core too. No one talks about them, no one remembers them, because they exist physically so they do not count. It's not perceived as assassination when people appear alive. They are assessed according to some official guidelines to determine their obvious handicaps, and maybe receive some reparations, as if what was done to them can be measured or repaired. What can be done? No one is asking this question.

Fifty years have passed, and this Holocaust disappears from people's memories, is reinvented by revisionists and deniers who miss the good old bloody days, and the new generations do not want to know about it. When we ask questions, we are told not to endlessly relive this catastrophe. We tire people with our life stories. Sometimes we suffocate them with our narratives. Or our silence. We are told that we cannot raise future generations on tragedies that happened so long ago.

Maybe they are right, but this attitude will bring this civilized world with all its progress to bigger and larger tragedies. No one will be ready, no one will be prepared, and no one will want to understand in what direction the world is going. It is clear that other genocides will happen. If possible, they will be more brutal than Hitler and his Nazism and more brutal than the distorted and dangerous ideas they implemented. It is enough for me to mention the Islamic fundamentalism which wants, and tries, and may conquer the world. They dominated Europe once, and they will be back, as a more organized, encompassing power. You can ask their leaders, they do not shy away from expressing their views, and they do not lie when it comes to these statements of intent. They have enough followers willing to commit suicide, and they are capable of anything. This is just an example; there are more. Beware!

All those who "survived" can tell you what happened during the war. They represent an important resource for the world. These are not futile stories. After many years, it is difficult to remember specific feelings and sentiments from that time. The mind has also blocked numerous incidents of terror, beatings and near-death experiences.

Clearly, thoughts depended on the place and time. But there was fear everywhere all the time. Fear was different only in the ghetto, because at least in the beginning it was possible, to a certain extent, to hide from the criminals. In the village with the peasants, fear was not constant, because I did not meet other people and no one saw me, especially at night.

Life was quieter in the villages. The real problem was that I was alone, isolated, and spoke little with the peasants. We had nothing in common. The isolation was often unbearable. It made people leave a safe hiding place and set out to look for someone to communicate and interact with. In addition, I was missing my family terribly and was concerned about their fate. There were people who left knowing in advance that they were facing the danger of death, but they were incapable of staying isolated for a long time. Isolation was non-existent in the camp, although we were all alone. We had no control there, and we could change nothing about our situation.

Fear was present day and night and was constant. Fear of selection, disease, lack of food, and some insane murderer. We were beaten by many people. By supervisors, barrack supervisors, work supervisors, the police and various other distorted creatures. Fear followed us everywhere and defined every moment.

Nonetheless, I never caught myself losing all hope and I never completely accepted that bitter fate. I always believed I would somehow manage to get out. I did not know when or how, but I believed my day would come. Those who lost hope, those who became apathetic, who did not believe in the future, who thought they would be unable to help themselves; they all fell. Without hope and belief in oneself, survival was not possible. Those with no hope let themselves sink further, they no longer showered, cleaned their clothes, no longer took the meager food rations, and that was their end. Those who became indifferent and apathetic lost all hope, and no one in such a predicament believed in a future for himself or for his people. This is partly why they are no longer with us.

Our moods depended on rumors and fluctuated accordingly. Rumors about food, supplies, clothing and other elements of our lives which we had zero control over.

During the war, I also had rare moments of calm. We would sit together, all young, and among us there were some religious people, who could not practice their religion with prayers, in keeping the traditions of the holidays, or in any visible way. We would not argue about religion, especially about the Jewish religion which in our eyes was the religion of the Chosen People.

The religious among us – most of us came from deeply religious homes – said there was no need to try and understand what god was doing, and that only god knew what was going on. Of course, most people had a different approach and there was no answer as to why this was happening to the Chosen People. If god chose to have us murdered, if god chose that we be humiliated, degraded, starved, beaten, tortured and traumatized, maybe we should not believe in such a god. How can a god allow this to take place? One and a half million children who had never sinned were massacred.

And what about the old religious people? Even practicing Jews who spent their whole lives studying the Torah and who believed in their hearts and souls that god was watching them were butchered. They went to meet death with a prayer on their lips, and they were forced to march to the gas chambers like everyone else.

Does this god have no compassion? Does he have no pity? How come he gave so much power to despicable murderers? How could he let them kill all the believers? Had he no pity for babies and children and those too weak to fight the monster? How could he not protect them from these heinous killers? When people were weak, the Germans and their happy assassins killed people in cold blood. Including Americans. This god was sitting somewhere watching our poor planet and did nothing to stop the genocide. How can I believe in such a god? Maybe there is no god. And maybe there is no one to believe in.

We argued endlessly and in the meantime we were being eliminated, exterminated and degraded, and there was no sign from anywhere that this would ever stop. This discussion continues to this day and, still, we have no answers. Those who were extremely religious never sought answers and never gave answers. Why was there an inquisition? Why was there such a Shoa? Their answer was always: it is god's wish and we cannot understand god's ways. They felt the same as they were marched towards the gas chambers and died while praying perishing for Kiddush Hashem.

Sadly, many regret they "won" the war, and that they did not die with all the others after all. Some disagree with me, but I believe many felt this way. Despite our hopes and our great fortitude, many of us cannot rid ourselves of this burdensome past. Many among us deny it because they are ashamed to admit this thought to be true, but I think we are broken human beings, physically and mentally, many of us live only for our families whom we do not want to hurt.

If a people like the Germans decide to follow a certain route, they will go ahead with their plans and nothing will stop them. If the "world" tries to stop them, then they might be slowed down, and that in itself is not easy nor sufficient. There is always someone ready to help plan another tragedy, someone acquiescing to it and supporting it, and participating in the murders just like the Germans had the Japanese, the Italians, the Spaniards, and of course the Austrians, the Croats, the Romanians, the Ukrainians, the Hungarians, the Slovaks, the French and many more. Too many more. They were certain Germany would win and that it was better to be on the winning side. No one took into account that they, too, would be slaughtered. How naive.

As usual, childish, naive America, with its generosity and kindness, wanted to help, and the American people indeed helped restore that very people who had caused so much pain and suffering. They got back on their feet quickly with the help of the Marshall Plan. Here, again, the murderer benefited from the help, not the victim. Is this political strategy? Maybe. But it is also no small encouragement to future criminals, because in this case crime paid. These countries can plan new crimes and do as they please, or as pleases a few with a crooked mind and a sick soul. The world forgets and will forget in the future too. Nothing will be learned.

Kurt Waldheim, the Austrian Nazi, was chosen as the free world representative, the General Secretary of the United Nations – that was his reward. No one prevented his nomination, no one mentioned his past and his crimes against humanity, and no one stopped his fellowmen from choosing him as their president, and they were proud of him and of themselves. Finally, may I add, no one flinched when Pope John Paul II gave him a medal of honor for his achievements. Who says crime doesn't pay?

Thousands, perhaps tens of thousands, of those murderers received refugee status and political asylum in democratic countries immediately after the war. Many countries sought to hire these criminals to plan weapons factories, create arsenals in German efficient ways, and wooed them for jobs and high positions. Highly placed officials reached out to them for help, although they were aware that they had committed very serious crimes against humanity. Nevertheless, they helped them flee Europe and run away from justice. How absurd.

There are many moralists in this world who want to teach us what can and cannot be done, but all these political and religious moralists must first go through what we went through before they can comment on anything. Among these, the Vatican, which served as a springboard for all these murderers and helped them reach South America, has no right to moralize. The church's collaboration with the Nazis is well known, not only vis-a-vis the Jews but also the Catholic Gypsies, on whose behalf the church did not budge. The Poles believe that the Vatican is god's deputy, and still nothing was done to stop the genocide. In Poland antisemitism was, and still is, the daily special. A Catholic Pole I once met said to me: "We, the Poles, drink antisemitism in our mother's milk, and if we don't get enough of it, we get more in the church."

Not that churches outside Poland love Jews so much. Of course, the Vatican never questioned their decision to protect the perpetrators after the war, Nazis and all. They also never divulged how much of the assets the Nazis stole from Jews are sitting in their vaults. Even the few Catholic monks who helped Jewish children escape hoped to convert them and indeed in many cases that is exactly what happened. The Catholic Church should forever be humiliated and ashamed of its behavior.

September 1, 1939 to May 5, 1945 represents 68 months. I do not know if there is hell after death, but I do know there is hell during life. I assume that those who experienced the war as I did still live it even today. The hell is never ending. Such a thing does not stop with liberation. We can never free ourselves from it. Ever.

The freed prisoners who had a place to go back to left the camp immediately. Those who stayed were transferred to the central camp, to better buildings, and the conditions changed and improved. All the political criminals were immediately imprisoned. A typhus outbreak killed many of us.

I saw no point in staying there, so I turned to the camp's office and asked for advice as to what to do with myself. A Jewish officer in the American military who spoke Yiddish asked me questions about where I was originally from, who I was etc. and then suggested that since I came from Poland, I should go back there. Each morning a bus was leaving from Mauthausen to Warsaw, and he thought I should go back to my homeland. There was no consideration given to the fact that my whole family had been slaughtered there, and what I had experienced there. There was no way I could go back. Some Jews who did go back ended up being murdered by Poles.

Obviously, the Americans had no clue and could not comprehend our predicament. Poland had become a big burial ground for my family, my people, and there was no reason for me to return there. Only danger awaited me there, as many Jews who "dared" to go back to their homes only to find that Poles had stolen them experienced; some of them were even killed.

The Americans could offer me no alternative except to stay in the camp. That I could not do. It was very sad. Many had left already. While they did not know what to expect, they went looking for family members. Some had families to go back to, but many had nowhere to go. I had no home to return to, like all Polish Jews. Our situation was gloomy and sad and tragic. We tried to get organized into a team, and five of us decided to leave the camp and go towards Vienna. Since there was a typhus outbreak in the camp, the Americans prevented us from leaving. We turned to the offices of the American army and were told not to leave the camp because we could infect the civilian population. This angered us greatly and after a few minutes we decided to leave the camp against the Americans' instructions, our new masters and guardians, who were more concerned about the Austrian Jew haters than us. We were not prepared to receive orders from anyone anymore. We had had enough.

Infecting the local population was the least of our problems, so we walked towards the gate of the camp. The Americans stopped us there and prevented us from leaving. We were told that if we tried to escape, they, the Americans, would shoot us. We replied that it did not scare us and that if they wanted to fire on us, we were ready to take this chance. We got away from the gate. We rolled a few barrels towards the fence which was no longer electrified. We climbed onto the barrels helping each other out, we were very light, and jumped to the other side. The American guards shot in our direction, but the bullets did not hit us. The five of us walked in the direction of the road and the station, and there we climbed onto the roof of a train. There was no space inside, but we were on our way to Vienna.

Nothing and nobody waited for us in Vienna. We found a tired city, a neglected and filthy place, but not in ruins. We did not know exactly where to turn, where to go. We parted, with each one going in a different direction to try and figure out who to turn to, where to get help, and then got back together again. We all had similar stories. Our conclusion was that there was nothing for us in Vienna, and we wondered where to go next, who to turn to, but had no answers. We knew we could not go back to Poland, there was nothing there for us except the dead. Silence fell upon us. We sat with our private thoughts, and then someone involuntary spluttered out these words: "Let's go home!"

Home? Where was home? Did any of us have a home? Tragically, it turned out that he meant Mauthausen. We got very excited, then we became paralyzed, and then all at once we started sobbing bitterly. Five young men – the oldest of us was 25 years old – sobbing, it is something you don't see every day. After this shock, we asked ourselves why we had had to suffer throughout the war only to have no place to go, no one to turn to, no one to help us, to guide us. We did not know if any organization could assist, we had nothing, no one to ask advice from, no address, young men without a present and a future with no one to care about us. We had no choice. We walked back sadly to the train station and returned to Mauthausen. What a tragedy. How could we go on living like this? What should we expect? Why did we suffer so greatly? Was this why we fought to stay alive all those years? It was sad and it enraged us. Weren't we sufficiently destroyed? Why this terrible punishment? How could we solve these problems?

We could barely stand on our two feet. On the day I left the camp, I was weighed. I weighed 35 kilograms. 35 kilograms. That is 77 pounds.

We had managed to survive five years of horrors that were impossible to describe, what would life be like now? How did one cope with it? We started losing hope and returned to the camp, where they barely let us in. We started regretting the fact that we remained alive. I thought that it would have been better had I just died at the beginning of the war. All this suffering and pain only to suffer more after the war had ended? Weren't the dead better off? Those who were slaughtered years ago did not have to reach our pitiful stage. Each question gave birth to another question, and each question was more horrifying than the one before. Where were the answers? There were none.

During the war, being part of a group had helped us survive, and there was the hope that it would be over. Now we had no hope. We wandered around like ghostly prisoners. We got food, some clothing.

This was no future for a normal person, for the 24-year-old man that I was. I had all my future ahead of me, and yet I could not go back to where I came from, it was all destroyed. The local population would not only reject me, but openly oppose my return. Poles were slaughtering Jews who returned. They still wanted a Jew-free Poland and would not absorb those very Jews from whom they had stolen their properties, and who had been part of the cultural fabric of Polish society prior to the war. The German manmade hell was a dream come true for the Poles. It would not be wise to go there, to go where no one wanted me. If I returned, my life would be in danger.

No one came up with an alternative to Poland. We discussed moving to Palestine, but we did not know how to go about it. I was sad. After a few days, some soldiers from the Jewish brigade arrived at the camp from Eretz Israel. I heard the same argument from them. They could not really help us, the only possibility was getting to Southern Italy through our own means and ingenuity and perhaps from there we could embark on a boat to Israel. We should be able to find a way, they said. It seemed to me like a poor plan, a risky and complex alternative to rotting at the camp, but we had no other option.

I left Mauthausen with two friends, Szachne Gerstein and someone else whose name I do not recall. Szachne and I remained together until we arrived at a refugee camp we had heard rumors about in Linz, a city in Austria. We would see each other in Israel many years later, through Leon Goldbaum.

There was a large refugee camp in Linz. When we left Mauthausen, we had no food, no clothing, nothing. We would get into the houses of Austrian peasants who refused to let us in, and we would take their clothing, including underwear, which we had not had for five years, even if they protested. They seemed afraid of us. We asked them to give us food, and we would take money if they had any. We would walk into bakeries and take bread. We did not ask them to give it to us. We took it. We filled a bag we had taken from a peasant.

In one of the places that had been conquered by the Russians, we asked to see the mayor. He put us up in a hotel filled with Russian officers. They gave us tickets, like coupons, to buy clothing in stores, two pairs of everything we needed, and food too. One of the Russian officers I met at that hotel was named Avram. I told him in Yiddish that I wanted to go to Russia. He asked why. "To live there. I am afraid to go back to Poland," I said. He took me aside and whispered to me: "Go to Israel, there are Jews there. There is antisemitism in Russia, Stalin is no better than Hitler." I later met him in Rome; he had defected like thousands of Jewish Russian soldiers. We then continued to Vienna where we went to a hotel and informed them that we would be staying there.

There were many refugees from all over Europe, Jews, Gypsies and Poles who did not want to return to their homeland under Russian communist influence. There were also Romanians, Hungarians and Italian POWs who had come from camps in Germany. They were waiting for trains to go back to Italy.

One day, we found out that a train would be taking the Italians back and the three of us decided to join them. This train ride was an extraordinary adventure, so to speak. We spent most of the ride on the roof or we would stand between the wagons so that they would not recognize us as foreigners, since we were afraid we would not be permitted to enter Italy. After two days we arrived in Modena where we were placed in Modena University. They had turned it into a refugee camp, and it turned out that there were tens of thousands of people there.

After a few days of recovery from being on the road, we decided to continue to Rome. We boarded an Italian military train and arrived at the central train station. Of course, we had no money for the train ride, but the Italians did not harass us. However, they took our clothing, so we arrived in Rome without clothes. We spent some time in Cine Città which had been transformed into a camp. It had previously been Italy's Hollywood, a cinema paradise. We had to prove we were camp "graduates".

We stayed there for a few months. There were large halls and we would sleep on the floor and received food, clothing and a lot of military uniforms from killed American soldiers. We would dress in the uniforms and go to various entertainment halls, supposedly as American soldiers. When Americans stopped us, we would say we were Polish soldiers.

In Rome, we went to the Red Cross, to the Joint, to the Polish Consulate, as well as to other organizations including UNRA (United Nations Relief Agency). There were refugees from all over Europe, and there were even former SS men. It was not much fun living there, but we had no choice. Simcha, a friend of mine, and I made two friends, Marila and Stefa, two Polish Jewish young women. We went to the opera and theater together. The first opera I saw was *Norma*. There was a theater at Piazza Venetia. We would see movies too. We would take blankets from the camp and sell them at the market to get Lirettas. We sold masses of things in that manner, which helped us survive.

After a while, we decided that the two girls would be better off moving to a monastery in town, located not far from the previous Jewish ghetto. The problem was that men were not allowed to enter. However, we would sneak into their rooms in the evenings. During the day we would look for work. We tried to study Italian and Hebrew, visit museums, and after a while the girls left for the United States and Canada and we joined a kibbutz in Italy in order to go to Israel later on. There was no other way.

We had to join a kibbutz, and we had to join the Labor party, even though that was not what I wanted to do. But we were badly in need of some semblance of a social life, and we thought of our future. Both were impossible without joining the kibbutz and the party. Gradually, we stopped talking about the past and focused on building a future. I had no connection with anyone and had to start building my future with my own hands without assistance. I did not understand the extent of my personal destruction at that time. I only started understanding and internalizing it much later.

After spending eight months at this kibbutz in Italy, we got transferred to somewhere around Milan, and were told to be ready to leave at any time. After a while, we were put on trucks by the Jewish brigade going to La Spezia – an Italian harbor. We boarded a ship, and it was immediately stopped by the Italian police. We were held at the harbor for a few weeks. We had to go on a hunger strike which lasted for ten days – over 1,000 people joined in. We found out that the Jewish brigade was organizing "illegal" voyages to Israel, and we faced many difficulties, but, finally, the British allowed us to immigrate legally, and on May 18, 1946, I arrived in Haifa, a port town in the north of Israel.

When I was at La Spezia, I had received a letter from an uncle who had left many years prior to the USA, and he asked me to wait until he could send me papers to come to America. I replied that I was heading to Israel to help build a Jewish state. I said that if I ever wanted to come visit him, I thought the British would let me travel whenever I wanted to. I was angry with my uncle because I felt he had not done enough to help the family before the war. He could have perhaps saved some family members, but he did not do anything as far as I know. I went to Israel not knowing what to expect. I knew I would face great challenges, but I was too young to understand what awaited me. Much later, facing difficulties I hadn't imagined, it was too late for me to leave, and I could not move to the United States for personal reasons.

After arriving in Eretz Israel, I thought my hardships were over. Little did I know how wrong I was. Not that it resembled the war years in any way, but I was naked and had nothing. No one could help me look towards a future and a life in a new land, a new culture and conditions that were unfamiliar to me. Everything was foreign, including the language and the mentality.

Today, 50 years later, I know that very few people can testify to the past, as the great majority are no longer alive. All the details that I forget will never be recovered or discovered. Time, I thought, will help the healing, but then it will be too late anyway, since none of us will be here to tell the story anymore. So I took it upon myself to try to confront my past, hoping that I will succeed, and I believe the day will come when these writings will see the light of day, and this dream of mine shall come true.

I hope it will bring the memorial to a close.

Until now, I never found the mental strength to deal with the pain, and I postposed the project endlessly. I knew how difficult it would be to relive this tragedy. Remembering that most of the corporate-owned death camps – as well as others – were erased from the face of the earth makes the catastrophe that took place there even harder to cope with.

When a few years ago we contacted the Polish Consulate in New York to help us locate and "visit" Skarzysko, the consul said: "Skarzysko is just a town. You are free to visit it." Upon our insistence, he finally muttered that there was a military installation, that he did not know about the Skarzysko-HASAG plant, and that we would need special permission to get in. He also promised he would help us get passes to this military fixture (which supposedly stands on the camp's grounds). But we never heard from him again. Despite numerous attempts to reach him, this consul never spoke with us again. It is a great testimony to what the Poles are all about with regard to Jews and their own heinous role during the war.

Mauthausen did become a museum but is neglected and undignified today. The Russian camp no longer exists and instead there is a small forest under which tens of thousands of human beings are buried because the crematoria were too busy to burn them. When I visited Mauthausen, I did not see any sign indicating what was under that forest, and there is no memorial. "You see, the Austrians don't have the budget to build memorials," the Mauthausen guide told us. He even refused to let me in until I proved I was once a "resident" there. Entrance is for organized groups only, except for past inhabitants of the camp.

It turned out that he had also been an inmate at the camp, a Mauthausen "graduate" so to speak. He had also been in Buchenwald, but I did not visit it, it is beyond where I am willing to step my foot. All the other camps were probably erased from the face of the earth and nothingness replaced them. No one will ever know what went on inside them. This is why it is crucial to tell that even in these small camps, many were slaughtered by human monsters.

The huge house is empty. I sit by myself and I write and I remember, and as I continue writing, I remember more, and my thoughts turn back to the past and something opens and memories long gone flow back into my head and flood me. The drops fall slowly and provide me with the long-forgotten details. Sometimes I think it will never stop.

These are things I do not want to remember, and still they are floating in my head and if they come back to haunt me, I'll have to write them down, it is perhaps an obligation to do so. Things do not come back chronologically as I wish, they are all mixed up, all the details intertwine and get confused. I make an effort to organize my thoughts and put some order into them so that a normal person can read and understand. Despite the complete silence, I cannot do this. It is difficult to order my thoughts and to write it all down. Or at least write down what I can recall.

I feel like I'm on another planet, and I must stop and drink some water because I am back in the camps and I am also hungry, and then someone is beating me. The glass of water helps me place myself back in the present, at home. No one is beating me now and I am not hungry, all I felt was an illusion but I live what I write and I hear screams from the police, yelling by the German Gestapo, the Ukrainian guards, they all want to annihilate me and put me in the gas chamber and the crematorium. My head is filled with these images and sounds, not even for a moment do I feel free, I am in another world. Like a movie it all shows up on a screen, and I am the main actor in this drama.

I am not sure my writings will add anything to the hundreds of books already written on the subject. Is there more to add? To my profound regret, I feel there is much to add, and not one detail is trivial. Some subjects were never covered, like many "small" stories and incidents, and as long as we are alive, it is our duty to tell what we experienced.

My specific focus is the "small" camps; no one pays attention or gives importance to concentration camps of 2,000 to 3,000 prisoners. Nothing is known or acknowledged about them. Very few survived, there is no one who can share anymore. The world must know about this terrible tragedy too. These camps were officially established as labor camps, but for all intents and purposes served as extermination camps, some without gas chambers or crematoria. Hundreds of thousands perished in them, from starvation, from disease, from beatings, from torture, from filth, from systematic murder.

They were small camps with many Russian POWs, Gypsies, Poles, Frenchmen, Jews and others from all over Europe. That was one year prior to the end of the war, after Skarzysko Kamienna. The Germans did not really care whether we were Jews or not and the suffering was our common denominator, with no discrimination to race, religion, or people. These camps no longer exist today. They were simply erased. These is no one to place a flower there, there are no tombs or memorials. There were hundreds of such small camps spread throughout Poland and Germany. All were owned by corporations who made money, helped the German war machine run, and helped fulfill the higher purpose, fully cooperating with the Reich, systematically and methodically murdering the Jewish people and others.

In 1988, when the Communist regimes started disintegrating, I decided it was time to face some of my most important nagging problems and return to visit my birth country and my birthplace Sochaczew. I knew in advance that the town was ruined and that I would not find my childhood home, certainly not my family. But one cannot take away someone else's imagination, and so I fantasized. I prepared myself for the trip to Warsaw, which was destroyed too. The Warsaw I knew no longer existed, but I decided to see it for myself anyway. Before traveling there, I had decided to erect a monument to the memory of the Sochaczew Jews, no matter what the difficulties may be. I saw it as a sacred duty, so I had to overcome all my inner difficulties and pain and organize this trip. I had previously sought the advice of some friends from Sochaczew who lived in Israel, and they supported the idea.

Immediately after I made my decision, I started burning up inside. Time was pressing. I was ready to face unknown officials and hostile populations; I knew I would face an uphill battle. There were no live Jews there at all, no one to help, and each day seemed to stretch out forever. I could not wait; it seemed as if my family was waiting for me. I informed my current family of my decision. But I was still restless. I could not calm myself down even for an instant. I felt so motivated and had to take immediate action.

The shock of my own decision took me back to 1939 and I could not face up to my thoughts. Maybe someone was alive after all. All my townspeople were waiting, my whole family was waiting for me there. I must fulfill my sacred duty. I must build a memorial for them all. I am the only one who can, physically and financially. And mentally. It is too much of a burden. I will be happy to do it.

All those years, I could not bring myself to think about ever returning to Poland, a Poland in an unpleasant political context. We knew before my departure that the Jewish cemetery which had existed in Sochaczew for 600 years had been desecrated. It was simply destroyed. There is not one complete tombstone, not one tomb except for that of Pinhas Weinberg who was murdered after the war when he returned with his wife to Sochaczew and ran for mayor of the city. I must add that he was a Zionist official prior to the war, and taught me that we must live in Eretz Israel, so what was he looking for in Poland? Even though I knew about the Poles destroying everything, I was still shocked to see the extent when I arrived. Complete and utter destruction, only because it was a Jewish cemetery, an image of the deep hatred the Poles felt towards Polish Jews. They simply completed what the Germans didn't finish.

From what I know now, there were two families from Sochaczew who managed to survive the war. One was the Szwiatlowski family who fled to Russia and managed to come to Israel where they had children, grandchildren and great grandchildren who are still alive. The other was the Pinchewski family. They had a bakery and managed to hide under it until the war ended. When they heard the Poles knew they were hiding, they found out who had spread rumors about them, left their hiding place at night, burned down the informer's house and spread their own rumor that the partisans were to blame and would burn the houses of other would-be informers. They repeated their actions on another occasion. And indeed, they remained alive. They were forced to flee after the war, and I do not recall what exactly happened to them.

I knew in advance I would not be welcomed with open arms and that the locals would not appreciate my visit. I had to prepare myself for a population that was foreign to me. Since there were no Jews in town anymore, why have a Jewish cemetery? That would be their logic. Because of the town's expansion, the ex-cemetery area was now part of the town. Land was expensive, and they would fight me. I did not expect things to go smoothly. My family had been spread between the Warsaw ghetto, Ozarow, villages around Sochaczew and camps like Majdanek, Treblinka, and, of course, Auschwitz. I do not know the exact details and it does not make my life easy not to know.

My wife decided to join me on this difficult trip although she does not speak or understand Polish. We left for Warsaw, via Vienna. On the bus that took us from the terminal to the plane headed for Warsaw I was tense, a bundle of nerves, all trembling and shaking. I could not control myself and I was unable to calm myself down. When I boarded the bus, I was shaking, when I sat down on the airplane, I was shaking. Obviously, this was not the first time I flew. I have taken hundreds of flights since 1964. Millions of kilometers of different flights to different destinations. But this time it was different. After the plane took off, I quieted down a bit. My willpower, strong as steel, took over and was triumphant. But when the plane landed, I could not get up. I had to tell myself there was nothing more important in life than what I was about to accomplish. The memorial must be built.

The terminal in Warsaw looked more like a barn than anything else. In ten minutes, we were at the hotel. The next day we went to Sochaczew.

It is shameful and disgraceful what the Poles did to the Jewish cemetery. The cemetery is surrounded by houses occupied by local residents. They slowly expanded and built on cemetery grounds. They also built chicken coops so the chicken could feed and grow above Jewish burial ground. They build roofs for their open garages, different types of warehouses, and used this land for their various needs. A fire engine was standing in the cemetery, being cleaned. Hundreds of empty bottles had been thrown on the ground and garbage littered it. The high school, which is adjacent, used the ground as a soccer field. When I saw this, I realized what I had to face.

I wondered about the Poles among whom my family had lived for generations, and how they were capable of using sacred ground like this, for their filth and sports. Don't they have any respect for the dead? Where is their self-respect? The Poles admired their own religion; is this what the Catholic Church has taught them? I am not a great student of Catholicism, but I am sure that it teaches them to respect others, especially the dead. Where are the moralists now? Where are the town's administrators? They probably hoped none of us would ever come back to see this and demand that it be changed. And here I come, and I speak Polish on behalf of Polish Jews, citizens alive in Israel and others who were born here and want to clean up the area, because the cemetery grounds belong to us. We will make sure it is clean and we will erect a memorial here and we will build despite your destruction.

A few of the Poles were shocked when they heard me. First, they did not understand what I wanted from them. I asked to meet the school principal, who was the deputy mayor as well as the head of the communist party. He said he only had five minutes for me. But the meeting lasted much longer and was very harsh. I did not hear expressions of love from this man. He was angry because of my demand that they stop playing soccer on the cemetery within two days. He was enraged, in fact. I asked him if he would have turned his mother's grave into a soccer field. He went insane. My wife, who was present at the meeting but did not understand a word of it, said she felt murder in this man's voice, and was afraid he would kill me. He was shocked when he heard that I was speaking on behalf of the organization of Sochaczew Jewish residents, who had the same rights as he did, although none of us would ever return to live on this blood-soaked land. Still, we would not give up our right to have this Jewish property cleaned up, and that was why I was there. For that reason, I also represented the dead, those slaughtered and burned in every possible way who could not speak for themselves, 5,000 or so Jews, residents of Sochaczew. After I had thanked him for his "patience" and "courtesy", and after I had expressed hope that he would cooperate with me, I promised him that I would return in a few days' time.

I came back two days later, and the land was clean. But that was only the beginning. It was urgent to fence in the area and start building the memorial.

When I returned to Israel, I immediately started to organize all the necessary details related to the monument for the dead. I collected the funds and engineered plans, and when my other Sochaczew friends agreed to it, I returned to Sochaczew to build it.

* * *

When my father was lying on a wooden board in the barracks of Mauthausen, barely able to move, only hours before he was freed by American forces, he had a dream. He dreamt that a friend took him to the gates of the cemetery in Sochaczew and showed him a very large tombstone, and said to him: this is your tombstone. My father woke up in terror.

Later on, much later, the memorial he built on the cemetery grounds in Sochanczew for the Jews who had been murdered fit the tombstone he saw in his dream. He had these words inscribed on the stone:

"Remember: The Jews of Sochaczew and its surroundings lived here for 600 years. They were annihilated by the Nazis, 1939-1945." - Ella Scheinwald

* * *

We built a fence around the perimeter of the cemetery after all the chicken coops were relocated and the various shacks removed. In July 1991 there was a ceremony, the unveiling of the memorial and a symbolic common grave made from broken Jewish tombstones that I had found scattered around the area.

One of the schoolteachers, Pavel, had taken it upon himself to amass those pieces of stone inscribed with Hebrew letters. He turned to me and said: "Mr. Scheinwald, take all the stones from me, and do something with them. I am old and I cannot live with them, and when I die, I will probably go to hell because of them." So I took them and erected a large grave near the memorial.

We invited all the necessary dignitaries to the ceremony, including the local priest who did not show up, and the mayor, who instead of participating sent his wife and his deputy. We also called the Israeli Embassy in Warsaw and asked them to send a representative from the Jewish State, someone to be present when the memorial was unveiled, and to give the ceremony an official stamp which would perhaps encourage the Poles not to vandalize the monument. We felt an Israeli presence was important and would send a strong message on this hostile land that we once shared. To my deep regret, they too found excuses not to join the ceremony. Maybe I was not important enough to them, maybe it was because there was no press. Humbled and humiliated, we went on with our ceremony anyway, and may they feel shame for how they treated us.

That was closure for me.

In 2015 this memorial was vandalized and desecrated with hateful antisemitic graffiti, one of which read the following:"the Holocaust never happened – smiley face." The local Poles blamed this repugnant act on Muslims. - Ella Scheinwald

The year is 1995. I know that most of the witnesses to the years 1939-1945 are gone.

My desire to write what happened was born on the wooden boards in Mauthausen when I still did not dare to dream that I would stay alive. But because of the bugs and the lice that crawled on my skin and ate me alive, drinking the last drop of blood left under my skin, I dreamed there was a better world outside, that everyone's world was better and that I simply was not born in the right place or the right time. I thought I was born in a location that experienced war, but that the outside world was better, that everything was good, and that people were kind, that they would listen and help if necessary.

Deep inside, I hoped they had been unable to reach us because the war prevented them from doing so. I fantasized that as soon as this brutal war was over, everything would get back to normal and things would be fine and the world would be open and welcome us anywhere we wanted to go. I dreamed that people would be interested in knowing what we had experienced, and that they would strive to connect with us and understand our plight.

Today, fifty years later, I have no such illusions. I have matured and I perceive life differently. I understand we all have our fate. And I do not blame those who would not listen. Each person has their own problems, and oftentimes they cannot face their own personal difficulties. Those who can help often will not do so. We can just imagine what would happen if people had the patience and the tolerance, how much better this world would be for all of us. Unfortunately, life is tough, and everything I wrote is true and real. All the events, descriptions, names, people, those still alive, most dead, are real. Nothing in this story is the fruit of my imagination. It is a human story.

For me, it is certainly a hard, painful story. It is difficult to understand such barbarism, how can anyone imagine such cruelty? Each person can only try to imagine as best they can knowing every word is true. Each person can try to understand the horror that a people of 80 million committed. A people with a culture rooted for hundreds of years smack in the middle of Europe. How can a people go so low? Many questions can be asked. Many will certainly remain unanswered. Maybe history will judge.

How did I stay alive? How can a person exist in hell for nearly six years and remain alive when so many died? It is hard to picture. During all those cruel years, I was not a work supervisor, I was not a policeman, I was not a kapo, and I did not hold any other title. I simply tried to disappear in the crowd.

I cannot explain, to others or to myself, why I survived, except that I managed to keep in contact with friends and we helped each other out as best we could. In addition, I never volunteered for anything. All I did, except trying to survive from one moment to the next, was do my work well, even excelling at it. I forced myself never to be conspicuous. Another significant aspect is that I arrived at the camp after an amount of prior suffering. I had already been a refugee twice, once from Sochaczew and then during my flight to the villages.

Suffering followed me, or rather waited for me as I gravitated to it. I had already been in the Warsaw ghetto where I had faced starvation and death. If one can get used to suffering, then I was used to it. It is easier to survive under these circumstances – when you are used to the suffering. The only thing one cannot get used to is the hunger. You do not suffer less because you are used to being hungry. You can never get used to starvation and hunger. It causes immense pain.

Towards the end of the war, I was very experienced. Maybe I was strong physically, and all these combined elements and my young age and internal fortitude contributed to my survival. Luck must have also played a role. How else did I escape the many selections? Although my long-term experience in the camps perhaps taught me how not to be selected, one cannot ignore the fact that many were murdered simply because they stood in the wrong place during assembly, stood in the wrong place during work, did not understand German, or did not understand what they were told to do. I had the advantage of being fluent in German. Those who lived separated, alone, as individuals, had no chance of survival. Having friends to console and support was crucial.

I wish to add that not once throughout my existence in the camps did I argue with anyone. I accepted whatever decision was made by the group. Did I give up? Maybe. Here I had no choice either. It was better to be wrong and alive than to be completely right but completely dead. I accepted my fate to survive and my will to survive was stronger than anything. I was willing to give up my honor and then some to stay alive. And what honor is there in a place like a camp? My purpose was to live, not to sacrifice others. I was ready to sacrifice a lot, and indeed I came out alive from that hell. That is not a good reason to write this book. The reason is that I hope people will read and know what happened there. The story is not complete and can never be fully complete. There are no ways, no words to tell everything.

I am afraid of the Germans' future role and actions. They succeeded in educating their future generation, the Hitler Jugend, who are now adults and grew up on these atrocious theories. What do their children believe in? Children who grew up with extermination and genocide worldviews. There is no doubt that as a people, and even as individuals, the Germans understand and acknowledge what they did to the people of Europe, especially to the Jews and the Gypsies. They know how they burned children and old people alive, the sick and frail, and how they had demonic inventions of destruction to make human beings suffer before their death; they were tortured and tormented before being thrown away like garbage or burned like refuse. This happened only 50 years ago. Today we hear the new generation of Germans claim that they, the new generation, should not be blamed for their fathers' sins. They do not want to feel part of this evil or accept blame for it. It is very strange.

While the Jews did not kill Jesus over 2,000 years ago, don't some still accuse us of killing him? Doesn't the church still falsely hold Jews responsible? Don't they remember and never forget? The fact that he was killed by Romans is meaningless to them. The fact that he was just one person, not millions, only one person, and a Jewish one at that, is being put aside. The fact that it happened thousands of years ago seems irrelevant, they have not forgotten nor forgiven the Jews for this alleged but untrue deed. They do not even care who killed Jesus, they just want to blame the Jews.

Of course, young Germans cannot be blamed for their fathers' collective and individual murders, and neither can we. These same people that tell us to forgive and forget the murders of millions that took place 50 years ago remember the killing of one person over 2,000 years ago.

We were there. We existed in their fathers' hell, every minute, every day. Not only did the Germans and their allies annihilate my generation, they also erased those older and younger. They affected the second and third generation "survivors" of this inhuman trauma.

Their hideous crimes will not be erased, cannot be erased from the minds and lives of all generations to come, children of survivors and their children and on and on. In many ways, the Germans killed many generations, and harmed the lives of those who grew up with parents of the Holocaust.

To state merely that one was not born yet, and therefore is not to blame, is a poor excuse and a ridiculous argument. The whole German people and their fellow European murderers must take responsibility for their actions, and this whole people must be held accountable for generations to come for the harm they have caused and the destruction they have brought upon so many families. The orgy of mass murder was not initiated and performed by one man alone, rather by millions hungry for bloodshed who supported and helped him carry out his "final solution" project.

Instead of complaining that we should not blame the younger generation of Germans, they must make an effort to understand, to be compassionate, to try and repair and help the generations of young Jews born with this curse, the curse of being a child of Holocaust survivors. Germans: it was your parents and your grandparents and your great-grandparents who murdered us.

In his book entitled *Post-Ugandan Zionism On Trial*, S.B. Beit Zvi explains that some Jewish leaders supported the idea that we went to die like cattle. When a group of Polish Jews arrived in Palestine from occupied Europe during the war and reported the atrocities that went on, no one listened to them. There were people who truly disbelieved that such monstrosities could take place. How could they believe it if the leadership did not listen?

The newspapers ignored it. It suffices to say that we can look at newspapers from Palestine and the USA from 1941 to 1943 to understand why the people thought the news from Europe were exaggerated and that the Jews were not being massacred. No one believed this was happening.

As the Germans were exterminating us, in Palestine they were denying the extent of it. They told readers not to accept the numbers of tens of thousands murdered. Millions! Instead of having the Germans deny their actions, Jewish newspapers in Palestine minimized the extent of the genocide. How different are these newspaper opinions from those of policemen and guards in the ghettos? Which is worse? These helped the Germans to kill, and these denied such killings were taking place. It is irrelevant whether we speak of 1,000 or 200,000 people.

In both cases, everyone cooperated. To calm and mislead the public in view of such a tragedy is an extremely serious act. Whole communities and nations were quiet instead of rising up; these masses were kept ignorant and silent. What can we demand of others? Of course, US Jews were paralyzed, but the Yeshuv in Palestine should have taken immediate measures because they represented fighters, and were organized for war; they were much more able than American Jews. If they had made moves to oppose Germany, perhaps the world Jewry would have joined them in their fight against the demon.

I have no doubt that it would have somewhat served as deterrent to the Germans. It would have limited the level of the killings. That is my opinion.

At the same time, the media should have told the truth instead of trying to calm the population. Their job is first and foremost to inform the public, not hiding and manipulating facts. Their decisions and actions – or lack thereof – caused an unforgivable loss and made the Germans' job easier. They knew the situation even before 1942, but it all became a bureaucratic matter, they kept the information secret and dear time was lost.

For three months the Jewish leadership prevented the publication of a notice pertaining to the extermination of Jews in Europe. These were three critical months. But even after that, no action was taken. Everyone was busy with telegrams and investigations, and nothing was being done. They hid facts and caused great damage. There is no doubt that the Jewish leadership was well aware of what was going in Poland and Russia in 1942, but they did not believe it and did not want to believe it. When they finally took things seriously, they did nothing.

Isaac Greenbaum, the first Minister of the Interior following the creation of the State of Israel, said that they all knew about the slaughter in August, but refrained from telling the public about it. Greenbaum had previously been a member of the Polish senate and was one of the Jewish leaders in Poland. In *Post-Ugandan Zionism On Trial*, he states: "Yesterday a delegation representing refugees from Poland arrived. They told me, you have to swear on behalf of the Jewish Agency that there will not be any calm until the slaughter stops and until we save the rest of the Jews. I did not reply. I will not swear. Maybe it is important, but it is not the most important thing I have to do." There is no need to comment further on this.

It should be noted that Isaac Greenbaum was the Head of the Relief Committee. Ben Gurion had appointed him to the position. Ben Gurion did not consider this job very important. He had better things to do. Greenbaum not only did nothing in his capacity as Head of the Relief Committee, but he also blamed everyone else for what was happening. On January 8, 1943 in the Moshav of the Vaad Hapoel Hazioni (the Zionist Committee's headquarters), he blamed the community for not doing anything, and he attacked Polish Jews. Their behavior, he claimed, made him ashamed and humiliated. People became rags, he said of Polish Jews.

I would like to ask this hero that he thought he was why he did not lift a finger to help. He could have returned and fought the murderers. But instead, he hid the truth from the community and from himself. He did not want to know what was going on. When there were no Jews left alive anymore, he made himself appear as a hero and blamed everyone else. When it was too late to do anything, then they were ready to jump and do something. In my estimation, they did nothing relevant to assist us, they were busy with meetings, conferences, endless discussions, bureaucracy, political intrigue and power struggles, and had no time to deal with what was actually important. Their problems were on which committee to serve, which position was better, and focused on this self-centered and self-serving pursuit, they had no time for us.

In October 1942, a week after Ben Gurion returned to Israel (then Palestine) from Europe, he met reporters in the halls of the Jewish Agency. In a conversation with local and foreign reporters, he answered every possible question but did not say one word about the Holocaust. He had nothing to say about it. He was our hope and we counted on him, but he had nothing to say about us. The Jewish leadership acted similarly as we were being murdered.

In another meeting of the Zionist Committee, on November 30, 1942, Ben Gurion addressed himself to the ghetto Jews and said that they would avenge us, the victims, and would save us from the Nazis and the diaspora and would take us all to our country, which was being built.

Who was "all"? Didn't he know that "all" had become very few? By 1942, a large part of "all" was dead and the rest rotted in hell and their hours and minutes were counted. Didn't he know? Or was he just pretending? We wanted to believe someone was taking care of us and wanted to see us alive someday. We thought someone would fight for the children, and women, and men, and the elderly.

American Jewish leadership made no efforts either and did not take actual measures to help. Perhaps they were watching the Jewish leadership in Palestine. We never heard Haim Weizmann pronounce anything on the matter either. He was already destined to be president of Israel. Except for his expressed opinion that Polish Jews were a speck of dust that must face its destiny, he did nothing to help his people.[6]

American Jews, despite their numbers and strength, despite their influence and abilities, chose to do nothing for us. Maybe some helped, but they were few and far between. There was no one to rally people or to organize a drive for assistance. Everyone became paralyzed while we were being systematically and enthusiastically murdered by the German nation and its allies. It is time to tell this truth. I doubt that American and Israeli leaders who did nothing to lend us a hand died content with themselves and their decisions. Some leaders would not hesitate to send a whole army to its death for a mere political seat, but they would do nothing to help even their own people if there was no political interest or reward. In light of this experience, I do not trust and never will believe politicians.

In *Three Days of Battle,* Stefan Grayek, who was one of the organizers of the Warsaw ghetto uprising, writes: "Until the ghetto was separated from the world, there was a corresponding connection with the outside world and the Aryan side of Warsaw, also with the neutral countries and the Allied forces. There were letters in secret codes with the Jewish Agency in Geneva, Switzerland. Dr. Silberstein and Nathan Dror were there on behalf of the Agency. They passed on information from Palestine and they received information as to what was going on."

A similar connection was operating with Jewish representatives in Turkey in Kosta, and there Vania Pomerantz and Haim Berless were active. In some cases, representatives from those countries arrived in Warsaw and even offered financial aid. Later on, the connection was through the official Polish underground, via London, where the Polish government was temporarily installed. There were also representatives from relief institutions from Israel and the World Congress. The information that came from Warsaw was clear about the extermination of Jews. The Jewish underground expected some action to be taken, but nothing happened. There is no need for a more truthful testimony. The Jewish leadership knew what was going on in Poland, more than we were led to believe.

Nevertheless, they pretended they were receiving inauthentic information and made the public passive to the real situation. Indeed, how are such monstrosities believable? It is beyond the imaginable to believe such a sickening, horrendous, atrocious state. And so they did not react, and so what could be expected of others? In the end, everyone had statements to make, and the superpowers threatened to punish the guilty after the war. There were many promises made for the future, but the Jewish people remained stuck with its own fate. Not only did the world abandon us, our own leaders did very little to help us.

I derive no pride from the impotence or strategic decisions of the Jewish and non-Jewish leadership who did not lift a finger to help and save us.

The disappointment is great. Perhaps they could have saved some people. Maybe not millions, but some. Although I am alive, I feel what those who were led to the gas chambers must have felt. Like them, I was on my way to death many times, and by some miracle, or miracles, I was saved, but they still managed to kill me.

Maybe we lived to tell the world what was not done, and what should have been done. It is shameful. I have no respect for such leaders, and I am ashamed of them.

There is not enough paper and there are not enough words in the universe, not enough physical power or mental endurance to describe and to tell all the atrocities we lived through. Meanwhile, no one was asking the Germans, let alone dictating to them, to stop the genocide. Most surprising is that Jewish leaders acted like everyone else, as if the tragedy did not touch them, and by their lack of action, they legitimized others' lack of action. After all this, how can we see it as other than betrayal and complicity?

I cannot conclude without raising the subject which I hear so much about. Often I am told: "If the situation was so bad, why didn't you rebel? You had nothing to lose, you were so helpless, you had no chance, so what's the point of suffering instead of rebelling, fighting and dying in battle with dignity? You were fearful and you went to the slaughterhouse like cattle." I have heard this a number of times.

First, the Jews could not revolt. It should be clear that we had no weapons and no way of getting weapons of any kind. We were Polish citizens, and were, in theory, protected by the state. Our leaders had fled when they realized the dangers facing them. Many had fled to Russia, some arrived in Switzerland. The head of the Judenrat in Warsaw saw the danger to Polish Jews and to his own life, and he committed suicide with his family. That meant the end of official Jewish leadership in Poland. If there was a guide or leader after that, no one heard of them or saw them until 1945 when the war ended. Why did they escape? Why did they disappear and run without warning the people and helping them save themselves? They left us to our fate. To me, they are traitors, not leaders.

They knew what would happen to us and left us. It is fair to assume that someone like Menachem Begin, who was just a few years older than me, had studied Law and dealt with politics, and knew the contents of *Mein Kampf*, and was connected to Jabotinski, knew more than me, and he escaped to save himself and his family (although he left without his parents). If they did not know, they still had to risk their lives and stay with us. Leaders must know how to lead their people in the face of danger, otherwise they are not true leaders. But what we perceived as our leadership did not help us and the important ones among them did not find time to take care of European Jews. I am referring particularly to the Jewish leadership in USA and Palestine. They delegated this work to the lower bureaucracy without providing them with the authority or the means to confront the situation.

The great majority of these leaders did not lose sleep over what was happening to us, did not miss a breakfast from worrying about their own people being massacred during the war. After the war, some of the refugees were gathered in camps in Germany. They sent people to check who these "survivor-creatures" were, and the bureaucrats who visited those post-war camps wrote a report saying that those alive seemed to be the scum of the earth. The refugees were not fit to be brought into Israel. This is well documented in other books such as *The Seventh Million* by Tom Segev.

Nonetheless, this "scum of the earth" was brought to Israel to fight the wars and they went happily and loyally and spilled their blood while in many cases they were the sole, the very last, survivor of their entire family and town. They had survived the horrors, they did not speak or understand Hebrew nor did they understand the local military culture or orders they received. They were sent to fight the wars and died for the sake and very existence of the state and Jewish homeland. We were considered anti-social, and there were even suggestions that the bureaucrats would select who was fit to be moved to Israel. Another selection. They had no pangs of conscience whatsoever.

When the day came to ask for reparations, they did not hesitate to put their hand out and demand money as the representatives of the Jewish people, a people for whom they did nothing. They did not even want to hear our opinions on this sensitive matter. After all, it was on our backs, so who cared? They took money from the murderous criminals, they took our "compensation" money and refused to distribute it to victims on whose behalf they signed reparation agreements and for whom the money was transferred. No one even asked our opinion. The Germans' victims were not entitled to one penny from the Germans themselves. There was a selection here too, some were entitled to receive funds and for others, the Jewish State became guardian of the funds and was responsible for the distribution. That group was also discriminated against.

Only in the past few years I have come to realize that there was some degree of cooperation between the Nazis and leaders worldwide, whether in silence, inaction, bureaucracy, lack of understanding as to the real situation or indifference and ignorance. These were the leaders we expected so much from, those we hoped would rally and defend us. But all we heard was silence and then criticism against us. Why we did not fight back. Why we were led like cattle.

This is haunting me to this day and will haunt me and us until we all die. It shows a complete and utter lack of empathy and understanding of the fierce and brutal circumstances imposed upon us. We are accused of what others wanted us to do but they themselves refused to do anything except criticize.

This is true for American Jewry as well – none of them lost a minute's sleep over their fellow men. The American government knew of the genocide and chose to ignore it. It was as if they relished the idea of Jews being exterminated. Not one of those who express criticism and judgement today was ever confronted with a similar situation of brutality and murder, and perhaps they cannot understand the power of the murderous machine of the "final solution" and the extent of collaboration from the Poles, Ukrainians, Austrians, Hungarians, French and others. Maybe they cannot grasp what and how it happened. We were children after all. Don't they want to know how we survived such hateful savagery alone and afraid, hungry and sick, alone on the planet, and fearing for our lives every minute of every day?

Remember, we did not complete our education because our

families were torn apart and taken away, and there was no one left to teach us. We were educated by murderers, criminals, distorted men and women who delighted in killing human beings while living perfectly normal lives with their own families. We became experts in how to avoid gas chambers and crematoria and no one thought to ask us after the war how to heal us, how to repair our broken souls, no one inquired how to help us cope with the loss, the trauma, the tragedy of it all. After the fact, people come up with ideas, pseudo-solutions and advice, but these were inexistent when problems needed to be solved on an immediate and urgent basis.

Why didn't we fight?

There were cases of rebellion, the Warsaw ghetto, Bialystok, Vilnius and even Treblinka and Auschwitz.

J.F. Steiner wrote in his book *Treblinka* that a Czech soldier arrived without his family to Treblinka and that the kapos told him about the gas chambers, but he did not believe them. Most of the Jews from Warsaw were gassed there. But the kapos eventually convinced him and he later headed an uprising and died fighting against the Germans. This uprising was in fact a collective suicide. Very few remained alive, but the camp was ultimately closed in 1943.

I am certain there were rebellions and fights in other places as well, and that all were crushed and no one stayed alive to testify to the heroic attempts to fight the German murderers, who had a whole nation behind them. Everyone who tried to riot or rebel was crushed and there is no memory of them. I would like to ask specifically how we could in our condition, with no weapons, diseased and starved to death, rise up and fight? Who would have helped us?

Certainly not the Poles who mostly denounced us, as if to be a Jew was a crime. It is not as if they could greatly assist us in an uprising, but it is well worth remembering that over two million non-Jewish Poles were also killed. They were also sent to extermination camps; their intelligentsia was wiped out as early as 1939 and 1940, and they did not exactly all live in wonderful conditions. They felt they lived on their own land and 70% of them were agricultural. The farmers could have helped us, but in most cases refused to do so. They also tried to rebel but only after the Jewish Warsaw ghetto rebellion, and only after the Soviet army was very close to Warsaw and they were sure of a Russian victory. They did not fare too well. Remember there were 30 million people, living in conditions far better than ours, that did not really rebel. So what could we have done?

And what did the Germans themselves do? A nation of 80 million people. Today, many of them claim they were against the Hitler regime at the time, so why did they remain silent? How come those who were truthfully opposed to this heinous regime did not organize an uprising against their own hateful, murderous, fascist regime? Instead, they collaborated. What about the Austrians? What did they do when the world decided, and they agreed, that they were a conquered land? Masses volunteered to fight alongside the Germans for a Germany that would dominate the world for the next 1,000 years.

The Russians were also violently destroyed; number wise, more so than the Jews. When whole armies arrived with their officers and soldiers, split into divisions, to extermination camps, they were murdered to the very last one. Did the Russians rebel? Was there the possibility of rebelling? Hundreds of thousands of Russians met their death, like thousands and thousands before them.

There was no value to life, the Germans decided we were less than cockroaches, and death was rampant. That was the ideology, dream and collective purpose of the Germans. Death dominated everything. There was no chance for an uprising, and in many cases, people preferred to die than to suffer the pain of torture in case they were caught with weapons – which were impossible to come by in the camps in any case. This is a degree and depth of suffering that no words can describe. The Germans were experts on pain. No one was able to cope with such a brutal machine. Thus no one can preach now.

How come only the Jews are accused of being led like cattle? What about the Poles? The Gypsies? The Russians? The political prisoners?

No person who did not experience Nazi Germany on their own skin can ever understand what was happening. The Jews did more than any other people to fight against the Germans, according to the means we had at the time. Although unarmed, we fought for survival, for our lives. We were young, we wanted to live, and no outside support was there for us. We were children, alone, with no leader or guide, and had to cope with unfathomable situations. It is easy to judge today, but those who do had no courage and no idea how to help us then. When a tragedy unfolds today in a family, when one member is hurt or dies of unnatural causes, the family is often destroyed from sorrow and pain. Multiply that by millions of Jewish families who were slaughtered under the most cruel circumstances, and no one can visualize the immensity of the catastrophe. In most cases, whole families were wiped out, not one soul remained alive. Sometimes only a handful of people or just one person survived from entire towns. How is it possible to imagine or comprehend?

The very leadership that did nothing to help us and ignored the tragedy that was engulfing us cannot justify its lack of action by putting the blame on us and saying we did not rebel. We are the only ones who knew the murderous German Satan. We did whatever we could to cope. No one can preach to us today. It takes a lot of nerve and vulgarity to question our actions or lack thereof or even our ability to react against that monster of a nation.

It started when the Germans barred us from trading and holding liberal professions, pushed us into ghettos and disempowered us from earning a living, thus starving us. As early at that, we started to wonder about the international community, and in our best-case scenario, we dared not dream of America rescuing us.

We could not comprehend the silence from American Jewry. When we realized that no US organization, Jewish or otherwise, was giving any sign of life, and none of them intervened, we were incredulous and shocked. There was no one to ask, so we asked ourselves why they weren't assisting us. It was crucial beyond the shadow of a doubt to organize a tremendous rescue mission, as only Americans are capable of doing. They have proved it many times.

The Germans considered the USA as neutral although the Americans supported Britain, and US embassies were still opened and operating throughout Europe. The American government was clearly aware of where the situation was heading. The USA chose to just sit and watch how everything developed and do nothing about it. If anything was done to assist us, we were not aware of it, nor did we benefit from it in any way. Had the Americans intervened to our defense in any way – not necessarily financially – there is no doubt that it would have forced the Germans to rethink their plans, strategy and implementation.

When in fact the USA superpower did not intervene in the war immediately, and was not prepared to help – and I am not referring solely to helping the Jews, but rather helping everyone under German occupation – the Germans proceeded unimpeded with its murderous policies and acts against humanity. The USA did not even attempt to moderate the Germans on their killing path. Their interest was to keep the USA uninvolved and there was an urgent need to exploit that vacuum. They knew that at that juncture, only one power was capable of overcoming them. That was America. But the Americans ignored developments in Europe, and any action – if any was taken – was insufficient and ill-timed. The Germans took it as a green light to continue with their plans. In fact, there were some American citizens in ghettos and extermination camps, but the Germans did not fear any repercussions from the USA, and there was none.

Today, we often witness what the USA can do on the world stage, and the sums of money invested in foreign assistance where there is a political, military or strategic interest. In any region that experiences instability or where a weak population is being undermined, the USA often uses taxpayers' dollars and even sacrifices its own soldiers in the interest of other nations, which may or may not be friendly to the USA. Sometimes, countries benefitting from US help despise the USA, which is repaid with contempt and hatred. Knowing this, our pain doubled. When all our love and sympathy was with the USA, its back was turned to us, at least temporarily.

There is no doubt that military operations later on caused the Nazi regime to fall and the war to end. But because there was no immediate reaction to the Germans' atrocities, they interpreted the American silence as acquiescence. As a consequence, other countries felt under no obligation to assist either. They were looking to the world superpower, who was silent and indifferent. The symbol of strength supported the Germans with their silence and inaction. And so the Germans had free reign to oil their killing machine.

The USA's silence enabled those fascists to wipe out anyone they wanted. The damage to entire populations is immeasurable and unbearable. Many Germans found asylum in large and respected countries who were well aware of their crimes against humanity and still harbored them willingly. They became the accomplices of these criminals. By accepting and embracing them, these countries as well as the Catholic Church carry the responsibility of crimes against humanity.

I know that some Allied officials investigated the Germans in Mauthausen. Some were arrested, put on trial and jailed. I am certain that this was not thoroughly conducted. Even in cases of crimes against humanity, there were political and other considerations resulting in the freedom of too many German perpetrators.

The Russians did a more methodical job. They, without many considerations, sent the criminals to Siberia and cleaned them out more effectively than the Americans, French and British. They also used them for espionage purposes, and sometimes brought them back to Russia. They saved them from certain death and employed them for their own national interests. To this day, the Germans have not been properly punished, and many of them have lived better lives than most of us. For them, unfortunately, genocide was worth it. Not only was there no punishment after the crimes, but they received help and support following their long-term systematic state-sponsored criminal rampage.

The Jewish leadership in America and Eretz Israel ought to be ashamed. They measured our tragedy in financial, economic and political terms without asking our opinion, without involving us, and benefiting from the catastrophe we were experiencing, they then blamed us for walking into the gas chambers like cattle.

Some American politicians expressed issues with Dr. Goebbels between 1933 and 1945. He especially targeted American politicians and was propagating the rumor that president Roosevelt was a Jew, that the White House was filled with Jews, and that the Jews wanted to control the world and lead it into war. There was no hint of truth in all of this. But US politicians became intimidated and proceeded to ignore the Jews in order to prove those claims were untrue. Sadly, to this day it sounds familiar, and fits old anti-Semitic rhetoric. They were not strong enough to face and counter Nazi propaganda and instead of fighting it, they went along by remaining passive to this misinformation. It is a paradox that the USA – and the Vatican that hypocritically preaches helping the weak – gave a hand to those who perpetrated crimes against humanity, those very criminals from whom the USA had liberated us.

Finally, the USA also paid a heavy price. Over 300,000 American soldiers died or were murdered as POWs. Had the USA gotten involved earlier, and had it not hesitated or played politics for so long, had it pressured Germany, I presume that it would have been possible to avoid such heavy casualties and much pain would have been prevented. Together, the world could have stopped and destroyed the Nazi monster. No reparations paid by Germany (I accepted none) can compensate for the losses. Following the war, America did not save one penny in its generous financial support of Europe, which was rebuilt with US dollars. USA invested billions to restore Germany itself. The Marshall Plan to rebuild Europe included over 15 billion dollars' worth of aid.

Instead, Germany should have been left to bleed and pay for the reconstruction of Europe; it should have been accountable for the damages and compensation to every European country. The money should not have come from US taxpayers but German taxpayers, who should have repaid the USA, all of Europe and us. The expenses and losses they caused should have encouraged the Americans to put pressure on them to make payments. And then some. Maybe that would have taught them a lesson. That was the minimum necessary.

In addition, Germany (and some Swiss banks, and the Vatican) should return the billions in assets stolen from their victims, whether in money, real estate, artworks, and so on. Poland must follow suit. The monetary burden should not have fallen on the USA which, though late, saved the world from a bigger tragedy. Without American involvement the Germans' conquest would have lasted longer and caused the destruction of entire peoples in addition to the Jews. Others would have become illiterate slaves. The same fate would have met the Russians, Poles, Ukrainians and others. American prevented a further escalation, and we must appreciate that. Paradoxically, the burden of restoring all of Europe was on the back of Uncle Sam. Ironically, the United States ended up paying more than its share. Had they become involved in the war earlier, the loss of life and money would have been greatly limited.

I thank the Americans for their help after the war. Only those who were personally affected can appreciate the extent of it.

The world must know not to go forward with genocidal plans. Destroying other people should not be on the radar of any nation. But we all know many countries still go ahead with impunity. Often, the USA is the one who volunteers to pay for everything.

By the time the Americans joined the war effort, it was too late for us. Certainly, it was too late for the Jewish people as a whole. We had hoped the war would end earlier. US involvement did little for us on an immediate basis. Victories in Africa and Asia meant nothing to us. Until their invasion of Europe in June 1944, our situation was worsening. When we heard of the invasion, we were hoping that things would change faster than they actually did.

For us, the war lasted five and a half years, and most of our people was exterminated and with them millions more. Those who escaped death were tired and exhausted and had very little hope for the future. Immediately after the war, more died in relative huge numbers and the desire to survive starting fading. Many did not see a purpose in living and gave up. That was the easy thing to do. When the stress of the war diminished, if someone gave up hope, there was a feeling of anticlimax and within a day or two or three, sometimes the same day, they would die.

Everything had happened too late. Too late for the millions exterminated and too late to shorten the war. All our hopes had been pinned on the Russians, though I was never among those who believed in communism. Communism was hated in my house, even if only for its anti-religious stance and its isolationist approach. It was clear that such a regime would not solve the world's problems. We also hated them because they had signed the Ribbentrop-Molotov agreement that empowered the Germans.

We did not understand how a communist leader who preached freedom, unity and equality of all people was capable of signing a treaty with a murderous regime. We knew at the time that Stalin was not exactly a model or symbol of honesty and morality and that he had murdered millions. At least, from the outside, he addressed people's rights and we were astounded. The hate towards them mounted. But we had no alternative. Having no choice, we wanted to believe in something and put all our hopes on the Russians. I remember a discussion we had one day, as we were trying to forget our empty stomachs. I told my friends that I would be willing to give up ten years of my life to live in Siberia in exchange for freedom and half a kilo of bread per day despite my hate of communism.

Finally, one day I heard a student being interviewed on the *Galey Tzahal* radio channel saying that he had visited Auschwitz, that he was "intellectually" impressed though not hurt as a Jew, and that he was not angry with anyone, that we must forget, that a long time had passed since the war, and that there was no need to learn about the Holocaust in schools. I know this is a prevalent view in some circles, including Jewish circles in America and elsewhere. I was ashamed when I heard this interview. Then I wondered if this young man was to be blamed for his ideas. Certainly not. This is the way he was raised.

The real heroes are those who stood up and confronted the Nazi murderers. It is not for anyone who wasn't there to be critical and to judge. We cannot give out grades. Those who did nothing have no right to speak. If you did not protest, stay silent now too. If you did not rise up against the Nazis then, say nothing now. If you did not believe that the extermination was happening as reported, admit your mistake and say nothing else. At least admit your mistake.

I felt further humiliated by the criticism and the judgement made against us victims when I arrived in Israel. I felt the locals were ashamed of us and considered us inferior to them. They did not desire to accept us among them. Many victims had lost their homes and did not find a new home in Israel. It is not the case for all Holocaust survivors, but even if it is true for a few people, it is a shame.

It is a fact that many "survivors" did not adapt to their new lives – they never did.

I no longer trust any leadership. What I could not achieve with my own fortitude, and by myself, will not be achieved.

No ceremonies once a year for Yom HaShoah will help.

Not enough was done to help us, and moralizing is utterly shameful and disrespectful.

Maybe someone will forgive you one day.

Once upon a time, there was a town in Poland, and about 5,000 Jews lived there. But they were erased from the face of the earth and there are no more Jews in Sochaczew, only a memorial for those the earth swallowed.

After 600 years of life in Poland, there are no more Jews there.

And I? I am merely a murdered person who breathes and can

move about. The world seems too small for me, maybe I would be better off on another planet.

After I arrived to Israel, I moved 21 times, I built four houses, but found no place for myself here on this earth.

For me, there was no happy ending.

When I was a child, I followed the participants in the parade given by the Sochaczew firefighters with my friends, stepping with the rhythm of the march music, our eyes filled with joy and pride, and our hearts excited about the future that was awaiting us. But this world is no longer, and really never was. We just did not know it yet.

---

1. Because the Poles had to provide a certain amount of food to the Germans, the Slotys or heads of villages would go from house to house and warn the Poles that if they did not fill their quotas, the Germans would burn their houses. That is why they entered the house that evening, except for the carriage driver, who stayed outside on the cart.
2. It is a slang word used in the camps to denote a person about to die. The knees constituted the widest part of their bodies and their hips formed a rectangular shape above their skeletal legs. Their elbows were the thickest part of their arm, their stomachs were sunk in. It was more of a skeleton, with the skin becoming even thinner than a transparent plastic wrap. A Muselmann could no longer stand, he cried all the time, was passive and words would flow out uncontrollably from his mouth. We all knew the time frame within an hour or two when a Muselmann would die.
3. This Pole had planned this "show" to get me back. I do not remember his name, but he was very tall, about 1,90 meters, his chest bent over forward, Pinchas Feinshtaat had convinced him to save me. When I was exchanged with someone else, I felt nothing. I wanted to live, not to die. I wanted to tell the world what had happened to me. I felt obligated to follow my mother's prophecy. I would not have fought for someone else to die instead of me.
4. Wendelgard von Staden: *Nacht über dem Tal / Darkness Over the Valley.*
5. This transport lasted for 17 days. I arrived to Mauthausen on April 28, 1945. Because of the Germans' disorganization at that point in time, they lacked cigarettes, food and clothing. When I arrived to Rome in 1945, I sent through the Red Cross three or four letters to the peasants on whose properties I had hidden, I sent a letter to the priest and to the concierge of

our yard in Sochaczew (it turned out later that our house and yard had all been burnt). To date, none of them replied to me.
6. Cf. *Perfidy* by Ben Hecht, pp. 28, 184). Perhaps this opinion helped shape the thoughts of leaders in Palestine and strengthened the indifference of the USA to our plight.

EPILOGUE

I have concluded my writings, and I want to examine what I have put down on paper as objectively as possible. When I read these pages, it feels like this story does not touch me. I am disconnected. I am shocked and appalled and I can hardly believe that it is me, me indeed, who went through all this. I ask myself how I found physical and mental endurance to survive it all. On the other hand, I am baffled and shocked by what brutes could perpetrate these acts, and how a whole people volunteered and rallied to perform these crimes against human beings, and easily managed to recruit others who helped them enthusiastically and without reservation. All of them bandied happily together to implement the theories of a gang of mad men. For years, they were busy exterminating human populations as if they were bugs. They continued with their killings although everyone knew they had already lost the war. They refused to stop the murders even when they were conquered.

In his book *The Rise and Fall of the Third Reich*, William L. Shirer writes: "In March 1945, the manufacturing of coal decreased to one fifth in comparison with the previous year, and only a small part could be transported on trains due to the heavy bombing of the Allied forces." I am wondering then where they found enough coal to transport me for 17 days with 2,500 other skeletons without water or food and without purpose until most of us died. Is this possible to understand? They did not give up. Such transports were taking place in multiple locations where the Germans retreated and aimlessly were transporting us shadows nowhere. Where did they find the coal, trains and manpower when they were in urgent need of each person to defend their murderous motherland? This was taking place from March 1945, the beginning of the end of the war. No normal human being can comprehend such madness.

Humanity must be wary in the future because mad men will rise again and people will support them, and they will bring tragedy to the world once more. In the end, they will fall victims to themselves, of course. But until they are destroyed, they will manage to erase other people. One must be vigilant and watch closely the tendencies of dictators who promise monstrosities and then keep their promises. They often know that they will meet their own demise. Still, people follow them blindly. Other manmade tragedies will unfold in the future, they did not end in 1945. We must be careful not to let these people repeat the same mistakes.

I am hopeful that the future will be brighter, but to my regret, I cannot truly believe it.

Let us hope, and let's be sure not to remain passive. We must work together to prevent new tragedies. A lot of leadership skills, intelligence, kindness, compassion and courage are needed. Is there such leadership today?

I ask of the new generation to be vigilant. I wish you much success. Open your eyes. And good luck.

AFTERWORD

When my father, Zeev Scheinwald, disembarked the boat in Israel, he was 26 years old. He was immediately given a gun and sent to Latrun to fight Israel's battles. He could barely stand on his two feet. He did not understand the language, the culture, the mentality. He was alone.

Later on, he married Lea Kuperschmidt, who had fled Poland and arrived in Israel with the "Teheran Children". They had a son together, Moshe. When he was a baby, Lea died of a brain tumor, leaving Zeev and Moshe alone.

In 1953, Zeev married Bruria Eisenstein who had a two-year-old daughter, Yael. Bruria had been a child in Romania during the Holocaust. Together Zeev and Bruria had two children. Doron, born 1967, and me.

My father lived and breathed the Holocaust and his personal tragedy every moment of his life. The bedtime stories he told me when I was a child were stories about his life and struggles, his sadness and losses. Some funny moments from his childhood featured too, and innocent, worry-free times only children experience.

Zeev worked as construction worker in the 1950s and 1960s. In the early 60s he received an offer to manage a large construction company in Cote d'Ivoire. We moved to Africa, where I had a beautiful childhood in paradise. A few years later we moved to Paris, and later on back to Israel.

Zeev became a self-made millionaire and philanthropist.

He was the kindest, strongest, and weakest man I have ever known.

He was my role model, and I loved him with all my heart and soul.

Ella Scheinwald

BIBLIOGRAPHY

Shabtai B. Beit Zvi, *Post-Ugandan Zionism On Trial*, Bronfman Publishers, Tel Aviv, 1997

Stephen (Shalom) Grayek, *Three Days of Battle*, Ministry of Defense, Israel, October 1972

Ben Hecht, *Perfidy*, in its Hebrew version, Dfuss Israel Be'am, 1985

Felicia Karai, *Death in Yellow*, in its original Hebrew version, Yad Vashem and Tel Aviv University, 1994

Tom Segev, *The Seventh Million*, in its original Hebrew version; 1991

Tom Segev, *The Israelis and the Holocaust*, Keter Publishing House, Jerusalem, 1992

William L. Shirer, *The Rise and Fall of the Third Reich*, Volume I and II, Simon & Schuster, New York, 1960 (in its French translation, Le Livre de Poche)

Sochaczew Journal, in Yiddish

Jean-Francois Steiner, *Treblinka,* in its original French version, Librairie Artheme Fayard, 1966

PHOTOS

Zeev on the right in the picture which was presumably taken in 1937 in Sochaczew with unknown individuals, the middle one could be his older brother

Zeev with Felix Houfouet Boigny, president of Cote d'Ivoire

Zeev with Felix Houfouet Boigny, president of Cote d'Ivoire

Zeev and his wife Bruria

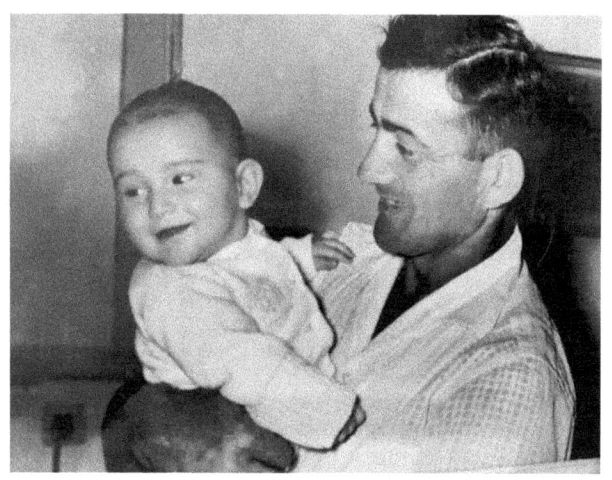

Zeev holding Ella

Ella inbetween her parents

Zeev at Rambam hospital where he donated the whole cardiac unit. The unit is named after Zeev's parents Lea and Moshe and his siblings

Zeev and grandchild Ronen

Zeev and granddaughter Dana

Ella with her husband and children

Entrance to the Jewish cemetery

Zeev (center) at Sochaczew memorial

Zeev picking stones local Poles broke from
Jewish tombstones to build a fence

Zeev walking along the field where the cemetery is in Sochaczew

Memorial dedication - Sochaczew (1991)

Memorial dedication - Sochaczew (1991)

Wall in Warsaw in the mid 1990s. The townhall
claimed they had no budget to clean it up

Memorial in Sochaczew. Copyright with www.shabbat-goy.com (Wikimedia)

Vandalized memorial - Sochaczew (2015)

Vandalized memorial - Sochaczew (2015)

Anti-semitic text on vandalized memorial - Sochaczew (2015)

ABOUT THE AUTHORS

Zeev Scheinwald was born on July 4, 1921 as Wolf (meaning Zeev in Hebrew) in Sochaczew, Poland.

When World War II broke out in 1939, he was taken prisoner and sent to various labor and concentration camps, while his entire family was exterminated by the Nazis and their collaborators.

He arrived in Israel in 1946, was enlisted in the military, and later worked in construction, over time becoming a successful building contractor.

He then moved with his family to Cote d'Ivoire in Africa where he headed a major construction company.

Later on, he moved with his wife and children to Paris.

Work brought them to many countries including Venezuela where he also led major construction projects.

Zeev became a successful businessman. He and his wife Bruria helped with numerous philanthropic causes.

He passed away in 2013.

* * *

Ella Scheinwald is an executive and management consultant and business strategist, and principal of NYC Advisors, LLC, a Management Consultancy firm.

Ella was previously USA Executive Director of Piguet International, a global credit reporting agency.

She graduated from the Sorbonne University in Paris and from MIIS (Middlebury) in California with Masters Degrees and a Post Graduate Degree in Languages and Linguistics, Intercultural Communications, International Policy Studies, Translating and Interpreting.

Ella grew up in Cote d'Ivoire, France and Israel. She has traveled extensively, and speaks four languages fluently.

She is a classical music piano player, loves giving piano recitals, traveling, reading, cooking and entertaining.

Ella lives in New York, is married and has two children.

Lightning Source UK Ltd.
Milton Keynes UK
UKHW011017050520
362811UK00002B/392